A Yankee in Canada

Henry David Thoreau

Foreword by

Richard F. Fleck

WESTWINDS
PRESS®

The Literary Naturalist Series

A Yankee in Canada was first published by Ticknor and Fields, Boston, 1866. Published with it in the same volume were Thoreau's collected Antislavery and Reform Papers.

Library of Congress Cataloging-in-Publication Data

Thoreau, Henry David, 1817-1862.
A Yankee in Canada / Henry David Thoreau.
    pages cm. — (The literary naturalist series)
Originally published: Montreal : Harvest House, 1961.
"First published by Ticknor and Fields, Boston, 1866"—Title page verso.
    ISBN 978-0-88240-922-1 (paperback)
    ISBN 978-1-943328-32-1 (hardbound)
    ISBN 978-1-943328-28-4 (e-book)
1. Québec (Province)—Description and travel. 2. Québec (Province)—Social life and customs—19th century. 3. Québec (Québec)—Description and travel. 4. Montréal (Québec)—Description and travel. 5. Thoreau, Henry David, 1817-1862—Travel—Québec (Province) 6. Americans—Travel—Québec (Province)—History—19th century. I. Title.
F1052.T48 2016
917.1404—dc23
                    2015024272

Designed by Vicki Knapton

Front cover photo: View of Beaver Hall Hill, with Craig Street in the foreground. On the left, one can see the Church of the Sion des Congrégationistes; in the center, St. Andrews Church, completed in 1851; and on the right, the cathedral—Lower Canada. Montréal, Québec, ca. 1851. Courtesy of Library and Archives Canada, Robert Lisle/Robert Lisle collection/c-047354.

WestWinds Press®
An imprint of

GRAPHIC ARTS
BOOKS®
P.O. Box 56118
Portland, OR 97238-6118
503-254-5591
www.graphicartsbooks.com

CONTENTS

Foreword by

RICHARD F. FLECK

Many critics, including Walter Harding, contend that Thoreau's reaction to Canada is narrow, provincial, and uninspired. Perhaps one could say that his inspiration, though not always, remained sequestered or secluded from his normal artistic impulse, and yet *A Yankee in Canada* remains interesting to us for just that reason. We see in this essay Thoreau's bare psyche and not the usual refined and polished artist of *Walden*, "Civil Disobedience," and other essays. Primal Thoreau transplanted to a foreign environment seems to have great difficulty in overcoming culture shock. Accordingly, his reactions to French Canada are mixed and ambivalent, which certainly affects his literary style. Generally he reacts unfavorably to Old World Catholicism, feudalism, and an alien British military presence. And generally all references to America and Americans are favorable. But if one looks closely he will see that positive reactions to Canadian society and negative reactions to American society do exist within the essay. In this sense *A Yankee in Canada* parallels Mark Twain's *Innocents Abroad* in that both authors are experiencing culture shock expressed with all the elements of a mental twilight zone of grays, not just black and white.

Thoreau's trip to Canada in 1850, three years after Walden Pond, however, is not his first experience with the impact of a different culture. His 1846 excursion to the Maine woods and Abenaki culture constitutes his first true experience with another people and the same year 1846 is for Thoreau another form of culture shock at his own country's arrogant militarism at the commencement of the Mexican Wars.

I think these factors (his first trip to the Maine woods and his protest against the wars in Mexico and slavery in the United States, which led him to an overnight stay in jail) are important contexts to consider when one examines his impressions of his 1850 excursion into French Canada, where he faced a third wave of alien exposure. Shabby, woebegone Abenakis (instead of healthy, vigorous "noble savages") and a shabby, immoral American government create, to say the very least, a troubled spirit in the person of Henry Thoreau about to set foot in the French-speaking, Roman Catholic province of a nation to the north.

Two years after the close of the disturbing Mexican Wars, Thoreau and William Ellery Channing, along with other American tourists, traveled by rail and then boat across Lake Champlain to New York State and Canada in late September and early October 1850. This excursion was recorded in *A Yankee in Canada,* first published serially in *Putnam's* in 1853. Walter Harding, in *The Days of Henry Thoreau,* comments: "*A Yankee in Canada* is the least successful of Thoreau's various excursions. He announced on the first page, 'I fear that I have not got much to say about Canada, not having seen much,' and most readers agree with him." But again, let us look closer at Thoreau's record of his French Canadian experiences.

Thoreau quite openly displays his strong prejudice against both Roman Catholicism and British colonial militarism. At times he appears to be only a notch or two above the most chauvinistic of super-patriots, a strange role indeed for him. Because he did not go to wilder sections of Canada, but immersed himself deep into French Canadian culture, he had to confront that most chauvinistic quality within himself, despite himself. While culture shock is, on the surface, a negative experience, it fosters growth within an individual however meanly a record of it is expressed. By confronting a foreign culture, Thoreau had to test his inner qualities of expansiveness, which is at least as difficult a task as protesting against a repressive American government. Truly, this book is a record of a nineteenth-century intellectual's painful growth through culture shock even if it is expressed in a gauche manner. If we truly wish to know the mind of Thoreau, we must see it at work under all conditions, including those of duress.

Turning to the text itself, we read that Thoreau traveled through the rich autumnal colors of New England, which, curiously, suggested "bloodshed, or at least a military life, like an epaulet or sash, as if it were dyed with the blood of the trees whose wounds it was inadequate to stanch." Such imagery artistically precedes his objection to the extreme military presence in Canada. His eyes are constantly on the lookout for a different kind of scenery in Canada and even the borderlands do not let him down: "The shores of Sorel, Richelieu, or St. John's River, are flat and reedy, where I had expected something more rough and mountainous for a natural boundary between two nations. Yet I saw a difference at once, in the few huts, in the pirogues on the shore, and as it were, in the shore itself. This was an interesting scenery to me, and the very reeds or rushes in the shallow water, and the tree-tops in the swamps, have left a pleasing impression."

The denizens of St. John's seemed like mere Old World peasants to Thoreau, lacking in ambition. He writes, "I thought that the Yankee, though undisciplined, had this advantage at least, that he especially is a man who, everywhere and under all circumstances, is fully resolved to better his condition essentially." Such a statement will be keynote in that everywhere in Canada, whether military or civilian, people seem to be somehow content with their lot, while Americans are always improving theirs. But is not too much material progress in America the very thing that drove Thoreau to Walden Pond? One usually "shoots from the hip" when experiencing culture shock. Thoreau continues,

"The Canadians here [were] a rather poor looking race, clad in gray homespun, which gave them the appearance of being covered with dust." Simplistic dress, of course, is one of Thoreau's key points in the chapter "Economy" of *Walden*. Again he is shooting from the hip at this strange new land. Perhaps, Thoreau conjectures, their poor state is due to the British military presence.

When Thoreau first views Montreal he most certainly *does* "see much." The following image is reminiscent of William Wordsworth's poetic impressions of London. "We could see merely a gleam of light there as from a cobweb in the sun. Soon the city of Montreal was discovered with its tin roofs shining afar. Their reflections fell on the eye like a clash of cymbals on the ear." But why does not Thoreau first focus on commanding Mount Royal rising high above the tin-roofed city with its lush, maple forest slopes? Thoreau proceeds not to the mountain but to the church of Notre Dame perhaps because it was something foreign and alien to him. He could easily have climbed Mount Royal and hiked along its forested paths (as did I a little over a hundred years later), but no, he goes to a Catholic church as though he wanted and expected to be shocked!

His reaction to the Cathedral of Notre Dame (La Reine du Monde) is indeed mixed. He states, "The Catholic are the only churches which I have seen worth remembering" because they have a sacred atmosphere like a "cave." Because American Protestant churches are only open on Sundays, such a "cave" as Notre Dame "is worth a thousand of our churches." Since one can pray no matter what day, Thoreau believes that this old edifice is conducive to meditation were it not for the priests "who have fallen far behind the significance of their symbols." Such a mixed reaction of praising the perpetually open Canadian church as sacred yet of criticizing the American Sunday-only churches and calling Canadian priests "oxen" and Yankee tourists entering their church "baboons" is typical of culture shock. Impressions and reactions come from all quarters of the mind when one is immersed into a foreign culture.

After Thoreau and his companions leave the cathedral, they walk the streets of Montreal to catch glimpses of Mount Royal rising beyond the town. But it is not Mount Royal that strikes Thoreau's fancy; it is, rather, the faces of some Sisters of Charity, devotees of those sacred caves: "We also met some Sisters of Charity, dressed in black, with Shaker-shaped black bonnets and crosses, and cadaverous faces, who looked as if they had almost cried their eyes out, their complexions parboiled with scalding tears; insulting the daylight by their presence, having taken an oath not to smile. By cadaverous I mean that their faces were like the faces of those who have been dead and buried for a year, and then untombed, with life's grief upon them, and yet for some unaccountable reason, the process of decay arrested." Thoreau did not "see much" in Canada? True, he didn't see boreal forests and the frozen Arctic tundra, but he saw something in the faces of those Sisters of Charity that he had never seen before.

Additionally Thoreau witnessed in Canada, particularly in Quebec City, the manifestation of the very thing he so vehemently attacked in his essay "Civil Disobedience," a standing military presence. The first two chapters, particularly "Quebec and Montmorenci" read in part like an extension of his 1847 essay "Civil Disobedience." Thoreau, after watching marching soldiers, writes, "The problem appeared to be how to smooth down all individual protuberances or idiosyncrasies, and make a thousand men move as one man, animated by one central will."

A standing military could give humankind an example

of how to achieve harmony, but harmony for a good purpose rather than an evil one: "They now put their hands, and partially perchance their heads, together, and the result is that they are the imperfect tools of an imperfect and tyrannical [colonial] government. But if they could put their hands and heads and hearts all together, such a co-operation and harmony would be the very end and success for which governments now exist in vain." For Thoreau the British-dominated Canadian government is obviously not working for the benefit of the citizenry. He points out that 28,000 French Canadians, as opposed to 8,000 British Canadians, are under British military control. The soldiers who carried guns at armed fortresses of Quebec, Thoreau believed, drew attention to themselves as potential victims of violence. Clearly this foreshadows the future violence seen in British India and later in Northern Ireland. It is no small wonder that Thoreau reacts so vehemently against the British standing army since such an army was finally defeated in America only eighty years earlier. So rather than being impressed with Quebec's fortresses and soldiers, he humorously arms himself with an umbrella and a bundle to assault the gates of Quebec in order to gather flowers, not bullets, from the open fields of the Plains of Abraham above the city and the swiftly flowing Saint Lawrence River.

Thoreau's reaction to the French Canadian language is essentially positive. He begins his second chapter with favorable impressions of poetic-sounding French: "About six o'clock we started for Quebec, one hundred and eighty miles distant by the river; gliding past Longueuil and Boucherville on the right, and Pointe-aux-Trembles, 'so called from having been originally covered with aspens,' and Bout de l'Isle, or the end of the island, on the left. I repeat these names not merely for want of more substantial facts to record, but because they sounded singularly poetic to my ears." The French language lends itself to wild space as English does not—if anything it profanes it. Later, near Sainte Anne de Beaupré Thoreau comments on the name La Rivière au Chien "which brought to my mind the life of the Canadian voyageur and coureur de bois, a more western and wilder Arcadia, methinks, than the world has ever seen; for the Greeks, with all their wood and river gods, were not so much qualified to name the natural features of a country as the ancestors of these French Canadians; and if any people had a right to substitute their own for the Indian names, it was they. They have preceded the pioneer on our own frontiers, and named the prairie for us. La Rivière au Chien cannot, by any license of language, be translated into Dog River, for that is not such a giving it to the dogs, and recognizing their place in creation as the French implies."

A bit later he writes: "As soon as you leave the States, these saintly names begin. St. John is the first town you stop at (fortunately we did not see it), and thence-forward, the names of the mountains, and streams, and villages reel, if I may so speak, with the intoxication of poetry;—*Chambly, Longueuil, Pointe aux Trembles, Bartholomy* [Barthélemy]. . . . I could not at once bring myself to believe that the inhabitants who pronounced daily those beautiful and, to me, significant names, lead as prosaic lives as we of New England." Thoreau's super chauvinism seems to have melted a bit. Though he had been in Canada only a few days, he had begun to compare this new country with his own. While he experiences poetry of place in Canada, he remembers only prosaic lives back in America. Even though our Yankee in Canada had difficulty in speaking and comprehending French (for instance, he asked "Y a-t-il une maison publique ici? –auberge we should have said"), he still felt that it was an altogether poetic tongue. Perhaps his chauvinism in this regard was not so much Yankee as it was that of his Norman French ancestry.

But the manner of these French Canadians was quite another matter for Thoreau. Their life style does elicit his Yankee chauvinism. He writes, "The population which we had seen the last two days, —I mean the habitants of Montmorenci County,—appeared very inferior, intellectually and even physically, to that of New England. In some respects they were incredibly filthy. It was evident that they had not advanced since the settlement of the country, that they were quite behind the age, and fairly represented their ancestors in Normandy a thousand years ago." Thoreau found himself in his own trap and quickly corrected his ludicrous attitude. He felt that the French were so slow to progress that rather than "Frenchifying" the Indians, the Indians "Indianized" the French. Witness the following switch from chauvinistic criticism to hearty praise, a characteristic so typical of undergoing culture shock: "Thus, while the descendants of the Pilgrims are teaching the English to make pegged boots, the descendants of the French in Canada are wearing the Indian moccasin still. French, to their credit be it said, to a certain extent respected the Indians [the Cree People] as a separate and independent people, and spoke of them and contrasted themselves with them as the English have never done. They not only went to war with them as allies, but they lived at home with them as neighbors." This is a real switch for Thoreau in such a short space from "intellectually inferior" to having the wisdom of "living with Indians as neighbors"!

The feudal and seignorial system of French Canadian society was yet another bone of contention for Thoreau. The British government (the one Thoreau so vehemently criticizes for its standing army) "has been remarkably liberal to its Catholic subjects in Canada, permitting them to wear their own fetters, both political and religious, as far as was possible for subjects." And he comments, "The French have occupied Canada, not udally, or by noble right, but feudally, or by ignoble right. They are a nation of peasants."

But a few pages later he becomes critical of his fellow Yankees: "If the Canadian wants energy, perchance he possesses those virtues, social and others, which the Yankee lacks, in which case he cannot be regarded as a poor man." *A Yankee in Canada* is a study in paradox, the paradox being due to a man stunned by his only international experience.

We should not necessarily condemn this essay as inartistic and chauvinistic but rather welcome it as an accurate account of a sometimes painful, sometimes awkward growth and change in Thoreau.

At last it should be mentioned that Thoreau did experience great joy in the wild parts of the Saint Lawrence River Valley. His description of a rainbow mist in the Chaudière Falls reminds one of the best of John Muir's prose: "I saw here the most brilliant rainbow that I ever imagined. It was just across the stream below the precipice, formed on the mist which this tremendous fall produced; I stood on a level with the keystone of its arch. It was not a few faint prismatic colors merely, but a full semi-circle, only four or five rods in diameter, though as wide as usual, so intensely bright as to pain the eye, and apparently as substantial as an arch of stone." One could say of Thoreau's Canadian experience overall that it opened his eyes to a cultural rainbow not previously seen.

—Richard F. Fleck

Denver, Colorado, 2015

An earlier version was presented as a lecture to the Japan Thoreau Society, Tokyo, 1984.

Further Commentary on *A Yankee in Canada*:

Berry, Edmund. "A Yankee in Canada." *Dalhousie Review*, 23 (1943).

Gertler, Maynard. "Introduction," *Henry Thoreau, A Yankee in Canada*. Montreal: Harvest House, 1961.

Harding, Walter. *The Days of Henry Thoreau*. New York: Alfred A. Knopf, 1965.

Harding, Walter and Michael Meyer. *The New Thoreau Handbook*. New York: New York University Press, 1980.

I

CONCORD TO MONTREAL

I fear that I have not got much to say about Canada, not having seen much; what I got by going to Canada was a cold. I left Concord, Massachusetts, Wednesday morning, September 25th, 1850, for Quebec. Fare, seven dollars there and back; distance from Boston, five hundred and ten miles; being obliged to leave Montreal on the return as soon as Friday, October 4th, or within ten days. I will not stop to tell the reader the names of my fellow-travellers; there were said to be fifteen hundred of them. I wished only to be set down in Canada, and take one honest walk there as I might in Concord woods of an afternoon.

The country was new to me beyond Fitchburg. In Ashburnham and afterward, as we were whirled rapidly along, I noticed the woodbine (*Ampelopsis quinquefolia*), its leaves now changed, for the most part on dead trees, draping them like a red scarf. It was a little exciting, suggesting bloodshed, or at least a military life, like an epaulet or sash, as if it were dyed with the blood of the trees whose wounds it was inadequate to stanch. For now the bloody autumn was come, and an Indian warfare was waged through the forest. These military trees appeared very numerous, for our rapid progress connected those that were even some miles apart. Does the woodbine prefer the elm? The first view of Monadnoc* was obtained five or six miles this side of Fitzwilliam, but nearest and best at Troy and beyond. Then there were the Troy cuts and embankments. Keene Street strikes the traveller favorably, it is so wide, level, straight, and long. I have heard one of my relatives, who was born and bred there, say that you could see a chicken run across it a mile off. I have also been told that when this town was settled they laid out a street four rods wide, but at a subsequent meeting of the proprietors one rose and remarked, "We have plenty of land, why not make the street eight rods wide?" and so they voted that

---

*Monadnock is a granite-domed peak outside of Keene, New Hampshire, rising to 3,165 feet.

it should be eight rods wide, and the town is known far and near for its handsome street. It was a cheap way of securing comfort, as well as fame, and I wish that all new towns would take pattern from this. It is best to lay our plans widely in youth, for then land is cheap, and it is but too easy to contract our views afterward. Youths so laid out, with broad avenues and parks, that they may make handsome and liberal old men! Show me a youth whose mind is like some Washington city of magnificent distances, prepared for the most remotely successful and glorious life after all, when those spaces shall be built over and the idea of the founder be realized. I trust that every New England boy will begin by laying out a Keene Street through his head, eight rods wide. I know one such Washington city of a man, whose lots as yet are only surveyed and staked out, and except a cluster of shanties here and there, only the Capitol stands there for all structures, and any day you may see from afar his princely idea borne coachwise along the spacious but yet empty avenues. Keene is built on a remarkably large and level interval, like the bed of a lake, and the surrounding hills, which are remote from its street, must afford some good walks. The scenery of mountain towns is commonly too much crowded.

A town which is built on a plain of some extent with an open horizon, and surrounded by hills at a distance, affords the best walks and views.

As we travel northwest up the country, sugar-maples, beeches, birches, hemlocks, spruce, butternuts, and ash trees prevail more and more. To the rapid traveller the number of elms in a town is the measure of its civility. One man in the cars has a bottle full of some liquor. The whole company smile whenever it is exhibited. I find no difficulty in containing myself. The Westmoreland country looked attractive. I heard a passenger giving the very obvious derivation of this name, West-more-land, as if it were purely American, and he had made a discovery; but I thought of "my cousin Westmoreland" in England. Every one will remember the approach to Bellows Falls, under a high cliff which rises from the Connecticut. I was disappointed in the size of the river here; it appeared shrunk to a mere mountain stream. The water was evidently very low. The rivers which we had crossed this forenoon possessed more of the character of mountain streams than those in the vicinity of Concord, and I was surprised to see everywhere traces of recent freshets, which had carried away bridges and injured the railroad, though I had heard nothing of it. In Ludlow, Mount Holly, and beyond, there is interesting mountain scenery, not rugged and stupendous, but such as you could easily ramble over—long narrow mountain vales through which to see the horizon. You are in the midst of the Green Mountains. A few more elevated blue peaks are seen from the neighborhood of Mount Holly, perhaps Killington Peak is one. Sometimes, as on the Western Railroad, you are whirled over mountainous embankments, from which the scared horses in the valleys appear diminished to hounds. All the hills blush; I think that autumn must be the best season to journey over even the *Green* Mountains. You frequently exclaim to yourself, what *red* maples! The sugar-maple is not so red. You see some of the latter with rosy spots on cheeks only, blushing on one side like fruit, while all the rest of the tree is green, proving either some partiality in the light or frosts, or some prematurity in particular branches. Tall and slender ash-trees, whose foliage is turned to a dark mulberry color, are frequent. The butternut, which is a remarkably spreading tree, is turned completely yellow, thus proving its relation to the hickories. I was also struck by the bright yellow tints of the yellow-birch. The sugar-maple is remarkable for its clean ankle. The groves of these trees looked like vast forest sheds, their branches stopping short at a uniform height, four or five feet from the ground, like eaves, as if they had been trimmed by art, so that you could look under and through the whole grove with its leafy canopy, as under a tent whose curtain is raised.

As you approach Lake Champlain you begin to see the New York mountains. The first view of the Lake at Vergennes is impressive, but rather from association than from any peculiarity in the scenery. It lies there so small (not appearing in that proportion to the width of the State that it does on the map), but beautifully quiet, like a picture of the Lake of Lucerne on a music-box, where you trace the name of Lucerne among the foliage; far more ideal than ever it looked on the map. It does not say, "Here I am, Lake Champlain," as the conductor might for it, but having studied the geography thirty years, you crossed over a hill one afternoon and beheld it. But it is only a glimpse that you get here. At Burlington you rush to a wharf and go on board a steamboat, two hundred and thirty-two miles from Boston. We left Concord at twenty minutes before eight in the morning, and were in Burlington about six at night, but too late to see the lake. We got our first fair view of the lake at dawn, just before reaching Plattsburg, and saw blue ranges of mountains on either hand, in New York and in Vermont, the former especially grand. A few white schooners, like gulls, were seen in the distance, for it is not waste and solitary like a lake in Tartary; but it was such a view as leaves not much to be said; indeed, I have postponed Lake Champlain to another day.

The oldest reference to these waters that I have yet seen is in the account of Cartier's discovery and exploration of the St. Lawrence in 1535. Samuel Champlain actually discovered and paddled up the Lake in July, 1609, eleven years before the settlement of Plymouth, accompanying a war-party of the Canadian Indians against the Iroquois. He describes the islands in it as not inhabited, although they are pleasant— on account of the continual wars of the Indians, in consequence of which they withdraw from the rivers and lakes into the depths of the land, that they may not be surprised. "Continuing our course," says he, "in this lake, on the western side, viewing the country, I saw on the eastern side very high mountains, where there was snow on the summit. I inquired of the savages if those places were inhabited. They replied that they were, and that they were Iroquois, and that in those places there were beautiful valleys and plains fertile in corn, such as I have eaten in this country, with an infinity of other fruits." This is the earliest account of what is now Vermont.

The number of French Canadian gentlemen and ladies among the passengers, and the sound of the French language, advertised us by this time that we were being whirled towards some foreign vortex. And now we have left Rouse's Point, and entered the Sorel River, and passed the invisible barrier between the States and Canada. The shores of the Sorel, Richelieu, or St. John's River, are flat and reedy, where I had expected something more rough and mountainous for a natural boundary between two nations. Yet I saw a difference at once, in the few huts, in the pirogues on the shore, and as it were, in the shore itself. This was an interesting scenery to me, and the very reeds or rushes in the shallow water, and the tree-tops in the swamps, have left a pleasing impression. We had still a distant view behind us of two or three blue mountains in Vermont and New York. About nine o'clock in the forenoon we reached St. John's, an old frontier post three hundred and six miles from Boston and twenty-four from Montreal. We now discovered that we were in a foreign country, in a station-house of another nation. This building was a barn-like structure, looking as if it were the work of the villagers combined, like a log-house in a new settlement. My attention was caught by the double advertisements in French and English fastened to its posts, by the formality of the English, and the covert or open reference to their queen and the British lion. No gentlemanly conductor appeared, none whom you would know to be the conductor by his dress and demeanor; but erelong we began to see here and there a solid, red-faced, burly-looking Englishman, a little pursy perhaps, who made us ashamed of ourselves and our thin and nervous countrymen—a grandfatherly personage, at home in his great-coat, who looked as if he might be a stage proprietor, certainly a railroad director, and knew, or had a right to know, when the cars did start. Then there were two or three pale-faced, black-eyed, loquacious Canadian French gentlemen there, shrugging their shoulders; pitted as if they had all had the small-pox. In the mean while some soldiers, red-coats, belonging to the barracks near by, were turned out to be drilled. At every important point in our route the soldiers showed themselves ready for us; though they were evidently rather raw recruits here, they manoeuvred far better than our soldiers; yet, as usual, I heard some

Yankees talk as if they were no great shakes, and they had seen the Acton Blues manoeuvre as well. The officers spoke sharply to them, and appeared to be doing their part thoroughly. I heard one suddenly coming to the rear, exclaim, "Michael Donouy, take his name!" though I could not see what the latter did or omitted to do. It was whispered that Michael Donouy would have to suffer for that. I heard some of our party discussing the possibility of their driving these troops off the field with their umbrellas. I thought that the Yankee, though undisciplined, had this advantage at least, that he especially is a man who, everywhere and under all circumstances, is fully resolved to better his condition essentially, and therefore he could afford to be beaten at first; while the virtue of the Irishman, and to a great extent the Englishman consists in merely maintaining his ground or condition. The Canadians here, a rather poor-looking race, clad in gray homespun, which gave them the appearance of being covered with dust, were riding about in caleches and small one-horse carts called charettes. The Yankees assumed that all the riders were racing, or at least exhibiting the paces of their horses, and saluted them accordingly. We saw but little of the village here, for nobody could tell us when the cars would start; that was kept a profound secret, perhaps for political reasons; and therefore we were tied to our seats. The inhabitants of St. John's and vicinity are described by an English traveller as "singularly unprepossessing," and before completing his period he adds, "besides, they are generally very much disaffected to the British crown." I suspect that that "besides" should have been a because.

At length, about noon, the cars began to roll towards La Prairie. The whole distance of fifteen miles was over a remarkably level country, resembling a Western prairie, with the mountains about Chambly visible in the northeast. This novel, but monotonous scenery, was exciting. At La Prairie we first took notice of the tinned roofs, but above all of the St. Lawrence, which looked like a lake; in fact it is considerably expanded here; it was nine miles across diagonally to Montreal. Mount Royal in the rear of the city, and the island of St. Helen's opposite to it, were now conspicuous. We could also see the Sault St. Louis about five miles up the river, and the Sault Norman still farther eastward. The former are described as the most considerable rapids in the St. Lawrence; but we could see merely a gleam of light there as from a cobweb in the sun. Soon the city of Montreal was discovered with its tin roofs shining afar. Their reflections fell on the eye like a clash of cymbals on the ear. Above all the church of Notre Dame was conspicuous, and anon the Bonsecours market-house, occupying a commanding position on the quay, in the rear of the shipping. This city makes the more favorable impression from being approached by water, and also being built of stone, a gray limestone found on the island. Here, after travelling directly inland the whole breadth of New England, we had struck upon a city's harbor—it made on me the impression of a seaport—to which ships of six hundred tons can ascend, and where vessels drawing fifteen feet lie close to the wharf, five hundred and forty miles from the Gulf; the St. Lawrence being here two miles wide. There was a great crowd assembled on the ferry-boat wharf and on the quay to receive the Yankees, and flags of all colors were streaming from the vessels to celebrate their arrival. When the gun was fired, the gentry hurrahed again and again, and then the Canadian caleche-drivers, who were most interested in the matter, and who, I perceived, were separated from the former by a fence, hurrahed their welcome; first the broadcloth, then the homespun.

It was early in the afternoon when we stepped ashore. With a single companion, I soon found my way to the church of Notre Dame. I saw that it was of great size and signified something. It is said to be the largest ecclesiastical structure in North America, and can seat ten thousand. It is two hundred and fifty-five and a half feet long, and the groined ceiling is eighty feet above your head. The Catholic are the only churches which I have seen worth remembering, which are not almost wholly profane. I do not speak only of the rich and splendid like this, but of the humblest of them as well. Coming from the hurrahing mob and the rattling carriages, we pushed aside the listed door of this church, and found ourselves instantly in an atmosphere which might be sacred to thought and religion, if one had any. There sat one or two women who had stolen a moment from the concerns of the day, as they were passing; but, if there had been fifty people there, it would still have been the most solitary place imaginable. They did not look up at us, nor did one regard another. We walked softly down the broad-aisle with our hats in our hands. Presently came in a troop of Canadians, in their homespun who had come to the city in the boat with us, and one and all kneeled down in the aisle before the high altar to

their devotions, somewhat awkwardly, as cattle prepare to lie
down, and there we left them. As if you were to catch some
farmer's sons from Marlboro, come to cattle-show, silently
kneeling in Concord meeting-house some Wednesday!
Would there not soon be a mob peeping in at the windows?
It is true, these Roman Catholics, priests and all, impress me
as a people who have fallen far behind the significance of
their symbols. It is as if an ox had strayed into a church and
were trying to bethink himself. Nevertheless, they are capa-
ble of reverence; but we Yankees are a people in whom this
sentiment has nearly died out, and in this respect we cannot
bethink ourselves even as oxen. I did not mind the pictures
nor the candles, whether tallow or tin. Those of the former
which I looked at appeared tawdry. It matters little to me
whether the pictures are by a neophyte of the Algonquin or
the Italian tribe. But I was impressed by the quiet religious
atmosphere of the place. It was a great cave in the midst of a
city; and what were the altars and the tinsel but the sparkling
stalactics, into which you entered in a moment, and where
the still atmosphere and the sombre light disposed to serious
and profitable thought? Such a cave at hand, which you can
enter any day, is worth a thousand of our churches which are

open only Sundays—hardly long enough for an airing—
and then filled with a bustling congregation—a church
where the priest is the least part, where you do your own
preaching, where the universe preaches to you and can be
heard. I am not sure but this Catholic religion would be an
admirable one if the priest were quite omitted. I think that I
might go to church myself sometimes some Monday, if I
lived in a city where there was such a one to go to. In Concord, to be sure, we do not need such. Our forests are such a
church, far grander and more sacred. We dare not leave *our*
meeting-houses open for fear they would be profaned. Such
a cave, such a shrine, in one of our groves, for instance, how
long would it be respected? For what purposes would it be
entered, by such baboons as we are? I think of its value not
only to religion, but to philosophy and to poetry; besides a
reading-room, to have a thinking-room in every city! Perchance the time will come when every house even will have
not only its sleeping-rooms, and dining-room, and talking-
room or parlor, but its thinking-room, also, and the archi-
tects will put it into their plans. Let it be furnished and orna-
mented with whatever conduces to serious and creative
thought. I should not object to the holy water, or any other

simple symbol, if it were consecrated by the imagination of the worshippers.

I heard that some Yankees bet that the candles were not wax, but tin. A European assured them that they were wax; but, inquiring of the sexton, he was surprised to learn that they were tin filled with oil. The church was too poor to afford wax. As for the Protestant churches, here or elsewhere, they did not interest me, for it is only as caves that churches interest me at all, and in that respect they were inferior.

Montreal makes the impression of a larger city than you had expected to find, though you may have heard that it contains nearly sixty thousand inhabitants. In the newer parts it appeared to be growing fast like a small New York, and to be considerably Americanized. The names of the squares reminded you of Paris—the Champ de Mars, the Place d'Armes, and others, and you felt as if a French revolution might break out any moment. Glimpses of Mount Royal rising behind the town, and the names of some streets in that direction, make one think of Edinburgh. That hill sets off this city wonderfully. I inquired at a principal bookstore for books published in Montreal. They said that there were none but school-books and the like; they got their books from the

States. From time to time we met a priest in the streets, for they are distinguished by their dress, like the civil police. Like clergymen generally, with or without the gown, they made on us the impression of effeminacy. We also met some Sisters of Charity, dressed in black, with Shaker-shaped black bonnets and crosses, and cadaverous faces, who looked as if they had almost cried their eyes out, their complexions parboiled with scalding tears; insulting the daylight by their presence, having taken an oath not to smile. By cadaverous I mean that their faces were like the faces of those who have been dead and buried for a year, and then untombed, with the life's grief upon them, and yet, for some unaccountable reason, the process of decay arrested.

> "Truth never fails her servant, sir, nor leaves him
> With the day's shame upon him."

They waited demurely on the sidewalk while a truck laden with raisins was driven in at the seminary of St. Sulpice, never once lifting their eyes from the ground.

The soldier here, as everywhere in Canada, appeared to be put forward, and by his best foot. They were in the proportion of the soldiers to the laborers in an African ant-hill. The inhabitants evidently rely on them in a great measure for music and entertainment. You would meet with them pacing back and forth before some guard-house or passage-way, guarding, regarding, and disregarding all kinds of law by turns, apparently for the sake of the discipline to themselves, and not because it was important to exclude anybody from entering that way. They reminded me of the men who are paid for piling up bricks and then throwing them down again. On every prominent ledge you could see England's hands holding the Canadas, and I judged by the redness of her knuckles that she would soon have to let go. In the rear of such a guard-house, in a large gravelled square or parade-ground, called the Champ de Mars, we saw a large body of soldiers being drilled, we being as yet the only spectators. But they did not appear to notice us any more than the devotees in the church, but were seemingly as indifferent to fewness of spectators as the phenomena of nature are, whatever they might have been thinking under their helmets of the Yankees that were to come. Each man wore white kid gloves. It was one of the most interesting sights which I saw in Canada. The problem appeared to be how to smooth down all individual protuberances or idiosyncrasies, and make a thousand men move as one man, animated by one central will; and there was some approach to success. They obeyed the signals of a commander who stood at a great distance, wand in hand; and the precision, and promptness, and harmony of their movements could not easily have been matched. The harmony was far more remarkable than that of any choir or band, and obtained, no doubt, at a greater cost. They made on me the impression, not of many individuals, but of one vast centipede of a man, good for all sorts of pulling down; and why not then for some kinds of building up? If men could combine thus earnestly, and patiently, and harmoniously to some really worthy end, what might they not accomplish? They now put their hands, and partially perchance their heads, together, and the result is that they are the imperfect tools of an imperfect and tyrannical government. But if they could put their hands and heads and hearts and all together, such a co-operation and harmony would be the very end and success for which government now exists in vain—a government, as it were, not only with tools, but stock to trade with.

I was obliged to frame some sentences that sounded

like French in order to deal with the market-women, who, for the most part, cannot speak English. According to the guide-book the relative population of this city stands nearly thus: two fifths are French Canadian; nearly one fifth British Canadian; one and a half fifth English, Irish, and Scotch; somewhat less than one half fifth Germans, United States people, and others. I saw nothing like pie for sale, and no good cake to put in my bundle, such as you can easily find in our towns, but plenty of fair-looking apples, for which Montreal Island is celebrated, and also pears, cheaper, and I thought better than ours, and peaches, which, though they were probably brought from the South, were as cheap as they commonly are with us. So imperative is the law of demand and supply that, as I have been told, the market of Montreal is sometimes supplied with green apples from the State of New York some weeks even before they are ripe in the latter place. I saw here the spruce wax which the Canadians chew, done up in little silvered papers, a penny a roll; also a small and shrivelled fruit which they called *cerises* mixed with many little stems somewhat like raisins, but I soon returned what I had bought, finding them rather insipid, only putting a sample in my pocket. Since my return, I find on comparison that it is the fruit of the sweet viburnum (*Viburnum Lentago*), which with us rarely holds on till it is ripe.

I stood on the deck of the steamer John Munn, late in the afternoon, when the second and third ferry-boats arrived from La Prairie, bringing the remainder of the Yankees. I never saw so many caleches, cabs, charettes, and similar vehicles collected before, and doubt if New York could easily furnish more. The handsome and substantial stone quay, which stretches a mile along the river-side, and protects the street from the ice, was thronged with the citizens who had turned out on foot and in carriages to welcome or to behold the Yankees. It was interesting to see the caleche drivers dash up and down the slope of the quay with their active little horses. They drive much faster than in our cities. I have been told that some of them come nine miles into the city every morning and return every night, without changing their horses during the day. In the midst of the crowd of carts, I observed one deep one loaded with sheep with their legs tied together, and their bodies piled one upon another, as if the driver had forgotten that they were sheep and not yet mutton. A sight, I trust, peculiar to Canada, though I fear that it is not.

II

QUEBEC AND MONTMORENCI

About six o'clock we started for Quebec, one hundred and eighty miles distant by the river; gliding past Longueil and Boucherville on the right, and *Pointe aux Trembles,* "so called from having been originally covered with aspens," and *Bout de l'Isle,* or the end of the island, on the left. I repeat these names not merely for want of more substantial facts to record, but because they sounded singularly poetic to my ears. There certainly was no lie in them. They suggested that some simple, and, perchance, heroic human life might have transpired there. There is all the poetry in the world in a name. It is a poem which the mass of men hear and read. What is poetry in the common sense, but a string of such jingling names? I want nothing better than a good word. The name of a thing may easily be more than the thing itself to me. Inexpressibly beautiful appears the recognition by man of the least natural fact, and the allying his life to it. All the world reiterating this slender truth, that aspens once grew there; and the swift inference is, that men were there to see them. And so it would be with the names of our native and neighboring villages, if we had not profaned them.

The daylight now failed us, and we went below; but I endeavored to console myself for being obliged to make this voyage by night, by thinking that I did not lose a great deal, the shores being low and rather unattractive, and that the river itself was much the more interesting object. I heard something in the night about the boat being at William Henry, Three Rivers, and in the Richelieu Rapids, but I was still where I had been when I lost sight of *Pointe aux Trembles.* To hear a man who has been waked up at midnight in the cabin of a steamboat, inquiring, "Waiter, where are we now?" is, as if at any moment of the earth's revolution round the sun, or of the system round its centre, one were to raise himself up and inquire of one of the deck hands, "Where are we now?"

I went on deck at daybreak, when we were thirty or forty miles above Quebec. The banks were now higher and more interesting. There was an "uninterrupted succession of white-washed cottages" on each side of the river. This is what every traveller tells. But it is not to be taken as an evidence of the populousness of the country in general, hardly even of the river banks. They have presented a similar appearance for a hundred years. The Swedish traveller and naturalist, Kalm, who descended this river in 1749, says: "It could really be called a village, beginning at Montreal and ending at Quebec, which is a distance of more than one hundred and eighty miles; for the farm-houses are never above five arpens,* and sometimes but three asunder, a few places excepted." Even in 1684 Hontan said that the houses were not more than a gun-shot apart at most. Erelong we passed Cape Rouge, eight miles above Quebec, the mouth of the Chaudière on the opposite or south side, New Liverpool Cove with its lumber rafts and some shipping; then Sillery and Wolfe's Cove and the Heights of Abraham on the north, with now a view of Cape Diamond, and the citadel in front. The approach to Quebec was very imposing. It was about six o'clock in the morning when we arrived. There is but a single street under

---

*One arpen (arpent) is equal to 0.84 acres.

the cliff on the south side of the cape, which was made by blasting the rocks and filling up the river. Three-story houses did not rise more than one fifth or one sixth the way up the nearly perpendicular rock, whose summit is three hundred and forty-five feet above the water. We saw, as we glided past, the sign on the side of the precipice, part way up, pointing to the spot where Montgomery was killed in 1775. Formerly it was the custom for those who went to Quebec for the first time to be ducked, or else pay a fine. Not even the Governor General escaped. But we were too many to be ducked, even if the custom had not been abolished.*

Here we were, in the harbor of Quebec, still three hundred and sixty miles from the mouth of the St. Lawrence, in a basin two miles across, where the greatest depth is twenty-eight fathoms, and though the water is fresh, the tide rises seventeen to twenty-four feet—a harbor "large and deep enough," says a British traveller, "to hold the English navy." I may as well state that, in 1844, the county of Quebec contained about forty-five thousand inhabitants (the city and suburbs having about forty-three thousand); about twenty-eight thousand being Canadians of French origin; eight thousand British; over seven thousand natives of

---

*Hierosme Lalemant says in 1648, in his relation, he being Superior: "All those who come to New France know well enough the mountain of Notre Dame, because the pilots and sailors, being arrived at that part of the Great River which is opposite to these high mountains, baptize ordinarily for sport the new passengers, if they do not turn aside by some present the inundation of this baptism which one makes flow plentifully on their heads."

Ireland; the rest Scotch and others. Thirty-six thousand belong to the Church of Rome.

Separating ourselves from the crowd, we walked up a narrow street, thence ascended by some wooden steps, called the Break-neck Stairs, into another steep, narrow, and zigzag street, blasted through the rock, which last led through a low massive stone portal, called Prescott Gate, the principal thoroughfare into the Upper Town. This passage was defended by cannon, with a guardhouse over it, a sentinel at his post, and other soldiers at the ready to relieve him. I rubbed my eyes to be sure that I was in the nineteenth century, and was not entering one of those portals which sometimes adorn the frontispieces of new editions of old black-letter volumes. I thought it would be a good place to read Froissart's Chronicles. It was such a reminiscence of the Middle Ages as Scott's novels. Men apparently dwelt there for security. Peace be unto them! As if the inhabitants of New York were to go over to Castle William to live! What a place it must be to bring up children! Being safe through the gate we naturally took the street which was steepest, and after a few turns found ourselves on the Durham Terrace, a wooden platform on the site of the old castle of St. Louis, still one hundred and fifteen feet below the summit of the citadel, overlooking the Lower Town, the wharf where we had landed, the harbor, the Isle of Orleans, and the river and surrounding country to a great distance. It was literally a *splendid* view. We could see six or seven miles distant, in the northeast, an indentation in the lofty shore of the northern channel, apparently on one side of the harbor, which marked the mouth of the Montmorenci, whose celebrated fall was only a few rods in the rear.

At a shoe-shop, whither we were directed for this purpose, we got some of our American money changed into English. I found that American hard money would have answered as well, excepting cents, which fell very fast before their pennies, it taking two of the former to make one of the latter, and often the penny, which had cost us two cents, did us the service of one cent only. Moreover, our robust cents were compelled to meet on even terms a crew of vile halfpenny tokens, and bungtown coppers, which had more brass in their composition, and so perchance made their way in the world. Wishing to get into the citadel, we were directed to the Jesuits' Barracks—a good part of the public buildings here are barracks—to get a pass of the Town Major. We did not heed the sentries at the gate, nor did they us, and what under the sun they were placed there for, unless to hinder a free circulation of the air, was not apparent. There we saw soldiers eating their breakfasts in their mess-room, from bare wooden tables in camp fashion. We were continually meeting with soldiers in the streets, carrying funny little tin pails of all shapes, even semicircular, as if made to pack conveniently. I supposed that they contained their dinners—so many slices of bread and butter to each, perchance. Sometimes they were carrying some kind of military chest on a sort of bier or hand-barrow, with a springy, undulating, military step, all passengers giving way to them, even the charette-drivers stopping for them to pass—as if the battle were being lost from an inadequate supply of powder. There was a regiment of Highlanders, and, as I understood, of Royal Irish, in the city; and by this time there was a regiment of Yankees also. I had already observed, looking up even from the water, the head and shoulders of some General Poniatowsky, with an enormous cocked hat and gun, peering over the roof of a house, away up where the chimney caps commonly are with us, as it were a caricature of war and military awfulness; but I had not gone far up St. Louis Street before

my riddle was solved, by the apparition of a real live Highlander under a cocked hat, and with his knees out, standing
and marching sentinel on the ramparts, between St. Louis
and St. John's Gate. (It must be a holy war that is waged
there.) We stood close by without fear and looked at him. His
legs were somewhat tanned, and the hair had begun to grow
on them, as some of our wise men predict that it will in such
cases, but I did not think they were remarkable in any
respect. Notwithstanding all his warlike gear, when I
inquired of him the way to the Plains of Abraham, he could
not answer me without betraying some bashfulness through
his broad Scotch. Soon after, we passed another of these crea-
tures standing sentry at the St. Louis Gate, who let us go by
without shooting us, or even demanding the countersign.
We then began to go through the gate, which was so thick
and tunnel-like, as to remind me of those lines in Claudian's
Old Man of Verona, about the getting out of the gate being
the greater part of a journey—as you might imagine yourself
crawling through an architectural vignette *at the end* of a
black-letter volume. We were then reminded that we had
been in a fortress, from which we emerged by numerous zig-
zags in a ditch-like road, going a considerable distance to

advance a few rods, where they could have shot us two or three times over, if their minds had been disposed as their guns were. The greatest, or rather the most prominent, part of this city was constructed with the design to offer the deadest resistance to leaden and iron missiles that might be cast against it. But it is a remarkable meteorological and psychological fact, that it is rarely known to rain lead with much violence, except on places so constructed. Keeping on about a mile we came to the Plains of Abraham—for having got through with the Saints, we come next to the Patriarchs. Here the Highland regiment was being reviewed, while the band stood on one side and played—methinks it was *La Claire Fontaine,* the national air of the Canadian French. This is the site where a real battle once took place, to commemorate which they have had a sham fight here almost every day since. The Highlanders manoeuvred very well, and if the precision of their movements was less remarkable, they did not appear so stiffly erect as the English or Royal Irish, but had a more elastic and graceful gait, like a herd of their own red deer, or as if accustomed to stepping down the sides of mountains. But they made a sad impression on the whole, for it was obvious that all true manhood was in the process of being drilled out of them. I have no doubt that soldiers well drilled are, as a class, peculiarly destitute of originality and independence. The officers appeared like men dressed above their condition. It is impossible to give the soldier a good education, without making him a deserter. His natural foe is the government that drills him. What would any philanthropist, who felt an interest in these men's welfare, naturally do, but first of all teach them so to respect themselves, that they could not be hired for this work, whatever might be the consequences to this government or that—not drill a few, but educate all. I observed one older man among them, gray as a wharf-rat, and supple as the Devil, marching lock-step with the rest who would have to pay for that elastic gait.

We returned to the citadel along the heights, plucking such flowers as grew there. There was an abundance of succory still in blossom, broadleaved golden-rod, buttercups, thorn-bushes, Canada thistles, and ivy, on the very summit of Cape Diamond. I also found the bladder-campion in the neighborhood. We there enjoyed an extensive view, which I will describe in another place. Our pass, which stated that all the rules were "to be strictly enforced," as if they were determined to keep up the semblance of reality to the last gasp, opened to us the Dalhousie Gate, and we were conducted over the citadel by a bare-legged Highlander in cocked hat and full regimentals. He told us that he had been here about three years, and had formerly been stationed at Gibraltar. As if his regiment, having perchance been nestled amid the rocks of Edinburgh Castle, must flit from rock to rock thenceforth over the earth's surface, like a bald eagle, or other bird of prey, from eyrie to eyrie. As we were going out, we met the Yankees coming in, in a body, headed by a red-coated officer called the commandant, and escorted by many citizens, both English and French Canadian. I therefore immediately fell into the procession, and went round the citadel again with more intelligent guides, carrying, as before, all my effects with me. Seeing that nobody walked with the red-coated commandant, I attached myself to him, and though I was not what is called well-dressed, he did not know whether to repel me or not, for I talked like one who was not aware of any deficiency in that respect. Probably there was not one among all the Yankees who went to Canada this time, who was not more splendidly dressed than I was. It would have been a poor story if I had not enjoyed some distinction. I had on my "bad-weather clothes," like

Olaf Trygesson the Northman, when he went to the Thing in England, where, by the way, he won his bride. As we stood by the thirty-two-pounder on the summit of Cape Diamond, which is fired three times a day, the commandant told me that it would carry to the Isle of Orleans, four miles distant, and that no hostile vessel could come round the island. I now saw the subterranean or, rather, "casemated barracks" of the soldiers, which I had not noticed before, though I might have walked over them. They had very narrow windows, serving as loop-holes for musketry, and small iron chimneys rising above the ground. There we saw the soldiers at home and in an undress, splitting wood—I looked to see whether with swords or axes—and in various ways endeavoring to realize that their nation was now at peace with this part of the world. A part of each regiment, chiefly officers, are allowed to marry. A grandfatherly, would-be witty Englishman could give a Yankee whom he was patronizing no reason for the bare knees of the Highlanders, other than oddity. The rock within the citadel is a little convex, so that shells falling on it would roll toward the circumference, where the barracks of the soldiers and officers are; it has been proposed, therefore, to make it slightly concave, so that they may roll into the centre, where they would be comparatively harmless; and it is estimated that to do this would cost twenty thousand pounds sterling. It may be well to remember this when I build my next house, and leave the roof "all correct" for bombshells.

At mid-afternoon we made haste down *Sault-au-Matelot* street, towards the Falls of Montmorenci, about eight miles down the St. Lawrence, on the north side, leaving the further examination of Quebec till our return. On our way, we saw men in the streets sawing logs pit-fashion, and afterward, with a common wood-saw and horse, cutting the planks into squares for paving the streets. This looked very shiftless, especially in a country abounding in water-power, and reminded that I was no longer in Yankee land. I found, on inquiry, that the excuse for this was, that labor was so cheap; and I thought, with some pain, how cheap men are here! I have since learned that the English traveller, Warburton, remarked, soon after landing at Quebec, that everything was cheap there but men. That must be the difference between going thither from New and from Old England. I had already observed the dogs harnessed to their little milk-carts, which contain a single large can, lying asleep in the gutters regardless of the horses, while they rested from their labors, at different stages of the ascent in the Upper Town. I was surprised at the regular and extensive use made of these animals for drawing, not only milk, but groceries, wood, &c. It reminded me that the dog commonly is not put to any use. Cats catch mice; but dogs only worry the cats. Kalm, a hundred years ago, saw sledges here for ladies to ride in, drawn by a pair of dogs. He says, "A middle-sized dog is sufficient to draw a single person, when the roads are good"; and he was told by old people, that horses were very scarce in their youth, and almost all the land-carriage was then effected by dogs. They made me think of the Esquimaux, who, in fact, are the next people on the north. Charlevoix says, that the first horses were introduced in 1665.

We crossed Dorchester Bridge, over the St. Charles, the little river in which Cartier, the discoverer of the St. Lawrence, put his ships, and spent the winter of 1535, and found ourselves on an excellent macadamized road, called *Le Chemin de Beauport*. We had left Concord Wednesday morning, and we endeavored to realize that now, Friday morning, we were taking a walk in Canada, in the Seigniory of Beauport, a foreign country, which a few days before had seemed almost as far off as England and France. Instead of rambling to Flint's Pond or the Sudbury Meadows, we found ourselves, after being a little detained in cars and steamboats—after spending half a night at Burlington, and half a day at Montreal—taking a walk down the bank of the St. Lawrence to the Falls of Montmorenci and elsewhere. Well, I thought to myself, here I am in a foreign country; let me have my eyes about me, and take it all in. It already looked and felt a good deal colder than it had in New England, as we might have expected it would. I realized fully that I was four degrees nearer the pole, and shuddered at the thought; and I wondered if it were possible that the peaches might not be all gone when I returned. It was an atmosphere that made me think of the fur-trade, which is so interesting a department in Canada, for I had for all head-covering a thin palm-leaf hat without lining, that cost twenty-five cents, and over my coat one of those unspeakably cheap, as well as thin, brown linen sacks of the Oak Hall pattern, which every summer appear all over New England, thick as the leaves upon the trees. It was a thoroughly Yankee costume, which some of my fellow-travellers wore in the cars to save their coats a dusting. I wore mine, at first, because it looked better than the coat it covered, and last, because two coats were warmer than one, though one was thin and dirty. I never wear my best coat on a journey, though perchance I could show a certificate to prove that I have a more costly one, at least, at home, if that were all that a gentleman required. It is not wise for a traveller to go dressed. I should no more think of it than of putting on a clean dicky and blacking my shoes to go a-fishing; as if you were going out to dine, when, in fact, the genuine traveller is going out to work hard, and fare harder— to eat a crust by the wayside whenever he can get it. Honest travelling is about as dirty work as you can do, and a man needs a pair of overalls for it. As for blacking my shoes in such a case, I should as soon think of blacking my face. I carry a piece of tallow to preserve the leather, and keep out the water; that's all; and many an officious shoe-black, who carried off my shoes when I was slumbering, mistaking me for a gentleman, has had occasion to repent it before he produced a gloss on them.

My pack, in fact, was soon made, for I keep a short list of those articles which, from frequent experience, I have found indispensable to the foot-traveller; and, when I am about to start, I have only to consult that, to be sure that nothing is omitted, and, what is more important, nothing superfluous inserted. Most of my fellow-travellers carried carpet-bags, or valises. Sometimes one had two or three ponderous yellow valises in his clutch, at each hitch of the cars, as if we were going to have another rush for seats; and when there was a rush in earnest, and there were not a few, I would see my man in the crowd, with two or three affectionate lusty fellows along each side of his arm, between his shoulder and his valises, which last held them tight to his back, like the nut on the end of a screw. I could not help asking in my mind, What so great cause for showing Canada to those valises, when perhaps your very nieces had to stay at home for want of an escort? I should have liked to be present when the customhouse officer came aboard of him, and asked him to declare upon his honor if he had anything but wearing apparel in them. Even the elephant carries but a small trunk on his journeys. The perfection of travelling is to travel without baggage. After considerable reflection and experience, I have concluded that the best bag for the foot-traveller is made with a handkerchief, or, if he study appearances, a piece of stiff brown paper, well tied up, with a fresh piece within to put outside when the first is torn. That is good for both town and country, and none will know but you are carrying home the silk for a new gown for your wife, when it may be a dirty shirt. A bundle which you can carry literally under your arm, and which will shrink and swell with its contents. I never found the carpet-bag of equal capacity, which was not a bundle of itself. We styled ourselves the Knights of the Umbrella and the Bundle; for wherever we went, whether to Notre Dame or Mount Royal, or the Champ-de-Mars, to the Town Major's or the Bishop's Palace, to the Citadel, with a bare-legged Highlander for our escort, or to the Plains of Abraham, to dinner or to bed, the umbrella and the bundle went with us; for we wished to be ready to digress at any moment. We made it our home nowhere in particular, but everywhere where our umbrella and bundle were. It would have been an amusing circumstance, if the Mayor of one of those cities had politely asked us where we were staying. We could only have answered, that we were staying with his Honor for the time being. I was amused when, after our return, some green ones inquired if we found it easy to get accommodated; as if we went abroad to get accommodated, when we can get that at home.

We met with many charettes, bringing wood and stone to the city. The most ordinary looking horses travelled faster than ours, or, perhaps they were ordinary looking, because, as I am told, the Canadians do not use the curry-comb. Moreover, it is said, that on the approach of winter their horses acquire an increased quantity of hair, to protect them from the cold. If this be true, some of our horses would make you think winter were approaching, even in midsummer. We soon began to see women and girls at work in the fields, digging potatoes alone, or bundling up the grain which the men cut. They appeared in rude health, with a great deal of color in their cheeks, and, if their occupation had made them coarse, it impressed me as better in its effects than making shirts at fourpence apiece, or doing nothing at all; unless it be chewing slate pencils, with still smaller results. They were much more agreeable objects, with their great broad-brimmed hats and flowing dresses, than the men and boys. We afterwards saw them doing various other kinds of work; indeed, I thought that we saw more women at work out of doors than men. On our return, we observed in this town a girl with Indian boots, nearly two feet high, taking the harness off a dog. The purity and transparency of the atmosphere were wonderful. When we had been walking an hour, we were surprised, on turning round, to see how near the city, with its glittering tin roofs, still looked. A village ten miles off did not appear to be more than three or four. I was convinced that you could see objects distinctly there much farther than here. It is true the villages are of a dazzling white, but the dazzle is to be referred, perhaps, to the transparency of the atmosphere as much as to the whitewash.

We were now fairly in the village of Beauport, though there was still but one road. The houses stood close upon this, without any front-yards, and at any angle with it, as if they had dropped down, being set with more reference to the road which the sun travels. It being about sundown, and the Falls not far off, we began to look round for a lodging, for we preferred to put up at a private house, that we might see more of the inhabitants. We inquired first at the most promising looking houses, if, indeed, any were promising. When we knocked, they shouted some French word for come in, perhaps *entrez,* and we asked for a lodging in English; but we found, unexpectedly, that they spoke French only. Then we went along and tried another house, being generally saluted by a rush of two or three little curs, which readily distinguished a foreigner, and which we were prepared now to hear bark in French. Our first question would be, *Parlez-vous*

Anglais? but the invariable answer was, *Non, monsieur;* and we soon found that the inhabitants were exclusively French Canadians, and nobody spoke English at all, any more than in France; that, in fact, we were in a foreign country, where the inhabitants uttered not one familiar sound to us. Then we tried by turns to talk French with them, in which we succeeded sometimes pretty well, but for the most part, pretty ill. *Pouvez-vous nous donner un lit cette nuit?* we would ask, and then they would answer with French volubility, so that we could catch only a word here and there. We could understand the women and children generally better than the men, and they us; and thus, after a while, we would learn that they had no more beds than they used.

So we were compelled to inquire: *Y a-t-il une maison publique ici?* (*auberge* we should have said, perhaps, for they seemed never to have heard of the other), and they answered at length that there was no tavern, unless we could get lodgings at the mill, *le moulin,* which we had passed; or they would direct us to a grocery, and almost every house had a small grocery at one end of it. We called on the public notary or village lawyer, but he had no more beds nor English than the rest. At one house there was so good a misunderstanding at once established through the politeness of all parties, that we were encouraged to walk in and sit down, and ask for a glass of water; and having drank their water, we thought it was as good as to have tasted their salt. When our host and his wife spoke of their poor accommodations, meaning for themselves, we assured them that they were good enough, for we thought that they were only apologizing for the poorness of the accommodations they were about to offer us, and we did not discover our mistake till they took us up a ladder into a loft, and showed to our eyes what they had been laboring in vain to communicate to our brains through our ears, that they had but that one apartment with its few beds for the whole family. We made our *a-dieus* forthwith, and with gravity, perceiving the literal signification of that word. We were finally taken in at a sort of public-house, whose master worked for Patterson, the proprietor of the extensive sawmills driven by a portion of the Montmorenci stolen from the fall, whose roar we now heard. We here talked, or murdered French all the evening with the master of the house and his family, and probably had a more amusing time than if we had completely understood one another. At length they showed us to a bed in their best chamber, very high to get into, with a low wooden rail to it. It had no cotton sheets, but coarse, home-made, dark colored, linen ones. Afterward, we had to do with sheets still coarser than these, and nearly the color of our blankets. There was a large open buffet loaded with crockery, in one corner of the room, as if to display their wealth to travellers, and pictures of Scripture scenes, French, Italian, and Spanish, hung around. Our hostess came back directly to inquire if we would have brandy for breakfast. The next morning, when I asked their names, she took down the temperance pledges of herself and husband, and children, which were hanging against the wall. They were Jean Baptiste Binet, and his wife, Geneviève Binet. Jean Baptiste is the sobriquet of the French Canadians.

After breakfast we proceeded to the fall, which was within half a mile, and at this distance its rustling sound, like the wind among the leaves, filled all the air. We were disappointed to find that we were in some measure shut out from the west side of the fall by the private grounds and fences of Patterson, who appropriates not only a part of the water for his mill, but a still larger part of the prospect, so that we were obliged to trespass. This gentleman's mansionhouse and grounds were formerly occupied by the Duke of

Kent, father to Queen Victoria. It appeared to me in bad taste for an individual, though he were the father of Queen Victoria to obtrude himself with his land titles, or at least his fences, on so remarkable a natural phenomenon, which should, in every sense, belong to mankind. Some falls should even be kept sacred from the intrusion of mills and factories, as water privileges in another than the millwright's sense. This small river falls perpendicularly nearly two hundred and fifty feet at one pitch. The St. Lawrence falls only one hundred and sixty-four feet at Niagara. It is a very simple and noble fall, and leaves nothing to be desired; but the most that I could say of it would only have the force of one other testimony to assure the reader that it is there. We looked directly down on it from the point of projecting rock, and saw far below us, on a low promontory, the grass kept fresh and green by the perpetual drizzle, looking like moss. The rock is a kind of slate, in the crevices of which grew ferns and golden-rods. The prevailing trees on the shores were spruce and arbor-vitae—the latter very large and now full of fruit—also aspens, alders, and the mountain-ash with its berries. Every emigrant who arrives in this country by way of the St. Lawrence, as he opens a point of the Isle of Orleans, sees the

Montmorenci tumbling into the Great River thus magnificently in a vast white sheet, making its contribution with emphasis. Roberval's pilot, Jean Alphonse, saw this fall thus, and described it, in 1542. It is a splendid introduction to the scenery of Quebec. Instead of an artificial fountain in its square, Quebec has this magnificent natural waterfall to adorn one side of its harbor. Within the mouth of the chasm below, which can be entered only at ebb tide, we had a grand view at once of Quebec and of the fall. Kalm says that the noise of the fall is sometimes heard at Quebec, about eight miles distant, and is a sign of a northeast wind. The side of this chasm, of soft and crumbling slate too steep to climb, was among the memorable features of the scene. In the winter of 1829 the frozen spray of the fall, descending on the ice of the St. Lawrence, made a hill one hundred and twenty-six feet high. It is an annual phenomenon which some think may help explain the formation of glaciers.

In the vicinity of the fall we began to notice what looked like our red-fruited thorn bushes, grown to the size of ordinary apple-trees, very common, and full of large red or yellow fruit, which the inhabitants called *pommettes,* but I did not learn that they were put to any use.

III

ST. ANNE

By the middle of the forenoon, though it was a rainy day, we were once more on our way down the north bank of the St. Lawrence, in a northeasterly direction, toward the Falls of St. Anne, which are about thirty miles from Quebec. The settled, more level, and fertile portion of Canada East may be described rudely as a triangle with its apex slanting toward the northeast, about one hundred miles wide at its base, and from two to three, or even four hundred miles long, if you reckon its narrow northeastern extremity; it being the immediate valley of the St. Lawrence and its tributaries, rising by a single or by successive terraces toward the mountains on either hand. Though the words Canada East on the map stretch over many rivers and lakes and unexplored wildernesses, the actual Canada, which might be the colored portion of the map, is but a little clearing on the banks of the river, which one of those syllables would more than cover. The banks of the St. Lawrence are rather low from Montreal to the Richelieu Rapids, about forty miles above Quebec. Thence they rise gradually to Cape Diamond, or Quebec. Where we now were, eight miles northeast of Quebec, the mountains which form the northern side of this triangle were only five or six miles distant from the river, gradually departing farther and farther from it, on the west, till they reach the Ottawa, and making haste to meet it on the east, at Cape Tourmente, now in plain sight about twenty miles distant. So that we were travelling in a very narrow and sharp triangle between the mountains and the river, tilted up toward the mountains on the north, never losing sight of our great fellow-traveller on our right. According to Bouchette's Topographical Description of the Canadas, we were in the Seigniory of the Côte de Beaupré, in the county of Montmorenci, and the district of Quebec; in that part of Canada which was the first to be settled, and where the face of the country and the population have undergone the least change from the beginning, where the influence of the States and of Europe is least felt, and the inhabitants see little or nothing of the world over the walls of Quebec. This Seigniory was granted in 1636, and is now the property of the Seminary of Quebec. It is the most mountainous one in the province. There are some half a dozen parishes in it, each containing a church, parsonage-house, grist-mill, and several sawmills. We were now in the most westerly parish called Ange Gardien, or the Guardian Angel, which is bounded on the west by the Montmorenci. The north bank of the St. Lawrence here is formed on a grand scale. It slopes gently, either directly from the shore, or from the edge of an interval, till, at the distance of about a mile, it attains the height of four or five hundred feet. The single road runs along the side of the slope two or three hundred feet above the river at first, and from a quarter of a mile to a mile distant from it, and affords fine views of the north channel, which is about a mile wide, and of the beautiful Isle of Orleans, about twenty miles long by five wide, where grow the best apples and plums in the Quebec District.

Though there was but this single road, it was a

continuous village for as far as we walked this day and the next, or about thirty miles down the river, the houses being as near together all the way as in the middle of one of our smallest straggling country villages, and we could never tell by their number when we were on the skirts of a parish, for the road never ran through the fields or woods. We were told that it was just six miles from one parish church to another. I thought that we saw every house in Ange Gardien. Therefore, as it was a muddy day, we never got out of the mud, nor out of the village, unless we got over the fence; then indeed, if it was on the north side, we were out of the civilized world. There were sometimes a few more houses near the church, it is true, but we had only to go a quarter of a mile from the road to the top of the bank to find ourselves on the verge of the uninhabited, and, for the most part, unexplored wilderness stretching toward Hudson's Bay. The farms accordingly were extremely long and narrow, each having a frontage on the river. Bouchette accounts for this peculiar manner of laying out a village by referring to "the social character of the Canadian peasant, who is singularly fond of neighborhood," also to the advantage arising from a concentration of strength in Indian times. Each farm, called *terre,* he says, is, in nine cases out of ten, three arpents wide by thirty deep, that is, very nearly thirty-five by three hundred and forty-nine of our rods; sometimes one half arpent by thirty, or one to sixty; sometimes, in fact, a few yards by half a mile. Of course it costs more for fences. A remarkable difference between the Canadian and the New England character appears from the fact that in 1745, the French government were obliged to pass a law forbidding the farmers or *censitaires* building on land less than one and a half arpents front by thirty or forty deep, under a certain penalty, in order to compel emigration, and bring the seigneur's estates all under cultivation; and it is thought that they have now less reluctance to leave the paternal roof than formerly, "removing beyond the sight of the parish spire, or the sound of the parish bell." But I find that in the previous or seventeenth century, the complaint, often renewed, was of a totally opposite character, namely, that the inhabitants dispersed and exposed themselves to the Iroquois. Accordingly, about 1664, the king was obliged to order that "they should make no more clearings except one next to another, and that they should reduce their parishes to the form of the parishes in France as much as possible." The Canadians of those days, at least, possessed a roving spirit of adventure which carried them further, in exposure to hardship and danger, than ever the New England colonist went, and led them, though not to clear and colonize the wilderness, yet to range over it as *coureurs de bois,* or runners of the woods, or as Hontan prefers to call them *coureurs de risques* runners of risks; to say nothing of their enterprising priesthood; and Charlevoix thinks that if the authorities had taken the right steps to prevent the youth from ranging the woods *(de courir les bois)* they would have had an excellent militia to fight the Indians and English.

The road, in this clayey looking soil, was exceedingly muddy in consequence of the night's rain. We met an old woman directing her dog, which was harnessed to a little cart, to the least muddy part of it. It was a beggarly sight. But harnessed to the cart as he was, we heard him barking after we had passed, though we looked anywhere but to the cart to see where the dog was that barked. The houses commonly fronted the south, whatever angle they might make with the road; and frequently they had no door nor cheerful window on the roadside. Half the time they stood fifteen to forty rods from the road, and there was no very obvious passage to them, so that you would suppose that there must be another road running by them. They were of stone, rather coarsely mortared, but neatly whitewashed, almost invariably one story high and long in proportion to their height, with a shingled roof, the shingles being pointed, for ornament, at the eaves, like the pickets of a fence, and also one row half-way up the roof. The gables sometimes projected a foot or two at the ridge-pole only. Yet they were very humble and unpretending dwellings. They commonly had the date of their erection on them. The windows opened in the middle, like blinds, and were frequently provided with solid shutters. Sometimes, when we walked along the back side of a house which stood near the road, we observed stout stakes leaning against it, by which the shutters, now pushed half open, were fastened at night; within, the houses were neatly ceiled with wood not painted. The oven was commonly out of doors, built of stone and mortar, frequently on a raised platform of planks. The cellar was often on the opposite side of the road, in front of or behind the houses, looking like an ice-house with us with a lattice door for summer. The very few mechanics whom we met had an old-Bettyish look, in their aprons and *bonnets rouges,* like fools' caps. The men wore commonly the same *bonnet rouge,* or red woollen or worsted cap, or sometimes blue or gray, looking to us as if they had got up with their nightcaps on, and, in fact, I afterwards found that they had. Their clothes were of the cloth of the country, *étoffe du pays,* gray or some other plain color. The women looked stout, with gowns that stood out stiffly, also, for the most part, apparently of some home-made stuff. We also saw some specimens of the more characteristic winter dress of the Canadian, and I have since frequently detected him in New England by his coarse gray homespun capote and picturesque red sash, and his well-furred cap, made to protect his ears against the severity of his climate.

It drizzled all day, so that the roads did not improve. We began now to meet with wooden crosses frequently, by the roadside, about a dozen feet high, often old and toppling down, sometimes standing in a square wooden platform, sometimes in a pile of stones, with a little niche containing a picture of the Virgin and Child, or of Christ alone, sometimes with a string of beads, and covered with a piece of glass to keep out the rain, with the words, *pour la vierge,* or *Iniri,* on them. Frequently, on the cross-bar, there would be quite a collection of symbolical knickknacks, looking like an Italian's board; the representation in wood of a hand, a hammer, spikes, pincers, a flask of vinegar, a ladder, &c., the whole, perchance surmounted by a weathercock; but I could not look at an honest weathercock in this walk without mistrusting that there was some covert reference in it to St. Peter. From time to time we passed a little one-story chapel-like building, with a tin-roofed spire, a shrine, perhaps it would be called, close to the pathside, with a lattice door, through which we could see an altar, and pictures about the walls; equally open, through rain and shine, though there was no getting into it. At these places the inhabitants kneeled and perhaps breathed a short prayer. We saw one school-house in our walk, and listened to the sounds which issued from it; but it appeared like a place where the process, not of enlightening, but of obfuscating the mind was going on, and the pupils received only so much light as could penetrate the shadow of the Catholic Church. The churches were very picturesque, and their interior much more showy than the dwelling-houses promised. They were of stone, for it was ordered, in 1609, that that should be their material. They had tinned spires, and quaint ornaments. That of l'Ange Gardien had a dial on it, with the Middle Age Roman numerals on its face, and some images in niches on the outside. Probably its counterpart has existed in Normandy for a thousand years. At the church of Chateau Richer, which is the next parish to l'Ange Gardien, we read, looking over the wall, the inscriptions in the adjacent churchyard, which began with, *"Ici git"* or *"Repose"* and one over a boy contained, *"Priez pour lui."* This answered as well as Père la Chaise. We knocked at the door of the curé's house here, when a sleek friar-like personage, in his sacerdotal robe, appeared. To our *Parlez-vous Anglais?* even he answered, *"Non, Monsieur";* but at last we made him understand what we wanted. It was to find the ruins of the old *chateau. "Ah! oui! oui!"* he exclaimed, and, donning his coat, hastened forth, and conducted us to a small heap of rubbish which we had already examined. He said that fifteen years before, it was *plus considérable.* Seeing at that moment three little red birds fly out of a crevice in the ruins, up into an arbor-vitae tree, which grew out of them, I asked him their names, in such French as I could muster, but he neither understood me nor ornithology; he only inquired where we had *appris à parler Français;* we told him, *dans les Etats-Unis;* and so we bowed him into his house again. I was surprised to find a man wearing a black coat, and with apparently no work to do, even in that part of the world.

The universal salutation from the inhabitants whom we met was *bon jour*, at the same time touching the hat; with *bon jour*, and touching your hat, you may go smoothly through all Canada East. A little boy, meeting us, would remark, "*Bon jour. Monsieur; le chemin est mauvais,*" Good morning, sir; it is bad walking. Sir Francis Head says that the immigrant is forward to "appreciate the happiness of living in a land in which the old country's servile custom of touching the hat does not exist," but he was thinking of Canada West, of course. It would, indeed, be a serious bore to be obliged to touch your hat several times a day. A Yankee has not leisure for it.

We saw peas, and even beans, collected into heaps in the fields. The former are an important crop here, and, I suppose, are not so much infested by the weevil as with us. There were plenty of apples, very fair and sound, by the roadside, but they were so small as to suggest the origin of the apple in the crab. There was also a small red fruit which they called *snells*, and another, also red and very acid, whose name a little boy wrote for me "*pinbéna.*" It is probably the same with, or similar to, the *pembina* of the voyageurs, a species of viburnum, which, according to Richardson, has given its name to many of the rivers of Rupert's Land. The forest trees were spruce, arbor-vitae, firs, birches, beeches, two or three kinds of maple, bass-wood, wildcherry, aspens, &c., but no pitch pines *(Pinus rigida)*. I saw very few, if any, trees which had been set out for shade or ornament. The water was commonly running streams or springs in the bank by the roadside, and was excellent. The parishes are commonly separated by a stream, and frequently the farms. I noticed that the fields were furrowed or thrown into beds seven or eight feet wide to dry the soil.

At the *Rivière du Sault a la Puce,* which, I suppose, means the River of the Fall of the Flea, was advertised in English, as the sportsmen are English, "The best Snipe-shooting grounds," over the door of a small public-house. These words being English affected me as if I had been absent now ten years from my country, and for so long had not heard the sound of my native language, and every one of them was as interesting to me as if I had been a snipe-shooter, and they had been snipes. The prunella or self-heal, in the grass here, was an old acquaintance. We frequently saw the inhabitants washing, or cooking for their pigs, and in one place hackling* flax by the roadside. It was pleasant to see

*Hackling is a process of combing out fiber (linen) from flax on a grooved board.

these usually domestic operations carried on out of doors, even in that cold country.

At twilight we reached a bridge over a little river, the boundary between Chateau Richer and St. Anne, *le premier pont de St. Anne,* and at dark the church of *La Bonne St. Anne.* Formerly vessels from France, when they came in sight of this church, gave "a general discharge of their artillery," as a sign of joy that they had escaped all the dangers of the river. Though all the while we had grand views of the adjacent country far up and down the river, and, for the most part, when we turned about, of Quebec in the horizon behind us, and we never beheld it without new surprise and admiration; yet, throughout our walk, the Great River of Canada on our right hand was the main feature in the landscape, and this expands so rapidly below the Isle of Orleans, and creates such a breadth of level horizon above its waters in that direction, that, looking down the river as we approached the extremity of that island, the St. Lawrence seemed to be opening into the ocean, though we were still about three hundred and twenty-five miles from what can be called its mouth.*

When we inquired here for a *maison publique* we were directed apparently to that private house where we were

---

*From McCulloch's Geographical Dictionary we learn that "immediately beyond the Island of Orleans it is a mile broad; where the Saguenay joins it, eighteen miles; at Point Peter, upwards of thirty; at the Bay of Seven Islands, seventy miles; and at the Island of Anticosti (about three hundred and fifty miles from Quebec) it rolls a flood into the ocean nearly one hundred miles across."

most likely to find entertainment. There were no guide-boards where we walked, because there was but one road; there were no shops nor signs, because there were no arti-sans to speak of, and the people raised their own provisions; and there were no taverns, because there were no travellers. We here bespoke lodging and breakfast. They had, as usual, a large old-fashioned, two-storied box-stove in the middle of the room, out of which, in due time, there was sure to be forthcoming a supper, breakfast, or dinner. The lower half held the fire, the upper the hot air, and as it was a cool Cana-dian evening, this was a comforting sight to us. Being four or five feet high it warmed the whole person as you stood by it. The stove was plainly a very important article of furniture in Canada, and was not set aside during the summer. Its size, and the respect which was paid to it, told of the severe win-ters which it had seen and prevailed over. The master of the house, in his long-pointed, red woollen cap, had a thoroughly antique physiognomy of the old Norman stamp. He might have come over with Jacques Cartier. His was the hardest French to understand of any we had heard yet, for there was a great difference between one speaker and another, and this man talked with a pipe in his mouth beside, a kind of tobacco

French. I asked him what he called his dog. He shouted *Brock!* (the name of the breed). We like to hear the cat called *min*—min! min! min! I inquired if we could cross the river here to the Isle of Orleans, thinking to return that way when we had been to the Falls. He answered, *"S'il ne fait pas un trop grand vent,"* If there is not too much wind. They use small boats, or pirogues, and the waves are often too high for them. He wore, as usual, something between a moccasin and a boot, which he called *bottes Indiennes,* Indian boots, and had made himself. The tops were of calf or sheep-skin, and the soles of cowhide turned up like a moccasin. They were yellow or reddish, the leather never having been tanned nor colored. The women wore the same. He told us that he had travelled ten leagues due north into the bush. He had been to the Falls of St. Anne, and said that they were more beautiful, but not greater, than Montmorenci, *plus beau, mais non plus grand que Montmorenci.* As soon as we had retired, the family commenced their devotions. A little boy officiated, and for a long time we heard him muttering over his prayers.

In the morning, after a breakfast of tea, maple-sugar, bread and butter, and what I suppose is called *potage* (potatoes and meat boiled with flour), the universal dish as we found, perhaps the national one, I ran over to the Church of La Bonne St. Anne, whose matin bell we had heard, it being Sunday morning. Our book said that this church had "long been an object of interest, from the miraculous cures said to have been wrought on visitors to the shrine." There was a profusion of gilding, and I counted more than twenty-five crutches suspended on the walls, some for grown persons, some for children, which it was to be inferred so many sick had been able to dispense with; but they looked as if they had been made to order by the carpenter who made the church. There were one or two villagers at their devotions at that early hour, who did not look up, but when they had sat a long time with their little book before the picture of one saint, went to another. Our whole walk was through a thoroughly Catholic country, and there was no trace of any other religion. I doubt if there are any more simple and unsophisticated Catholics anywhere. Emery de Caen, Champlain's contemporary, told the Huguenot sailors that "Monseigneur the Duke de Ventadour (Viceroy), did not wish that they should sing psalms in the Great River."

On our way to the Falls, we met the habitans coming to the Church of La Bonne St. Anne, walking or riding in charettes by families. I remarked that they were universally of small stature. The toll-man at the bridge over the St. Anne was the first man we had chanced to meet, since we left Quebec, who could speak a word of English. How good French the inhabitants of this part of Canada speak, I am not competent to say; I only know that it is not made impure by being mixed with English. I do not know why it should not be as good as is spoken in Normandy. Charlevoix, who was here a hundred years ago, observes, "The French language is nowhere spoken with greater purity, there being no accent perceptible"; and Potherie said "they had no dialect, which, indeed, is generally lost in a colony."

The falls, which we were in search of, are three miles up the St. Anne. We followed for a short distance a foot-path up the east bank of this river, through handsome sugar-maple and arbor-vitae groves. Having lost the path which led to a house where we were to get further directions, we dashed at once into the woods, steering by guess and by compass, climbing directly through woods, a steep hill, or mountain, five or six hundred feet high, which was, in fact, only the bank of the St. Lawrence. Beyond this we by good luck fell into another path, and following this or a branch of it, at our

discretion, through a forest consisting of large white pines—
the first we had seen in our walk—we at length heard the
roar of falling water, and came out at the head of the Falls of
St. Anne. We had descended into a ravine or cleft in the
mountain, whose walls rose still a hundred feet above us,
though we were near its top, and we now stood on a very
rocky shore, where the water had lately flowed a dozen feet
higher, as appeared by the stones and drift-wood, and large
birches twisted and splintered as a farmer twists a withe.
Here the river, one or two hundred feet wide, came flowing
rapidly over a rocky bed out of that interesting wilderness
which stretches toward Hudson's Bay and Davis's Straits.
Ha-ha Bay, on the Saguenay, was about one hundred miles
north of where we stood. Looking on the map, I find that the
first country on the north which bears a name is that part of
Rupert's Land called East Main. This river, called after the
holy Anne, flowing from such a direction, here tumbled over
a precipice, at present by three channels, how far down I do
not know, but far enough for all our purposes, and to as good
a distance as if twice as far. It matters little whether you call
it one, or two, or three hundred feet; at any rate, it was a sufficient Water-privilege for us. I crossed the principal channel

directly over the verge of the fall, where it was contracted to about fifteen feet in width by a dead tree, which had been dropped across and secured in a cleft of the opposite rock, and a smaller one a few feet higher, which served for a hand-rail. This bridge was rotten as well as small and slippery, being stripped of bark, and I was obliged to seize a moment to pass when the falling water did not surge over it, and midway, though at the expense of wet feet, I looked down probably more than a hundred feet, into the mist and foam below. This gave me the freedom of an island of precipitous rock, by which I descended as by giant steps, the rock being composed of large cubical masses, clothed with delicate close-hugging lichens of various colors, kept fresh and bright by the moisture, till I viewed the first fall from the front, and looked down still deeper to where the second and third channels fell into a remarkably large circular basin worn in the stone. The falling water seemed to jar the very rocks, and the noise to be ever increasing. The vista down stream was through a narrow and deep cleft in the mountain, all white suds at the bottom; but a sudden angle in this gorge prevented my seeing through to the bottom of the fall. Returning to the shore, I made my way down stream through the forest to see how far the fall extended, and how the river came out of that adventure. It was to clamber along the side of a precipitous mountain of loose mossy rocks, covered with a damp primitive forest, and terminating at the bottom in an abrupt precipice over the stream. This was the east side of the fall. At length, after a quarter of a mile, I got down to still water, and, on looking up through the winding gorge, I could just see to the foot of the fall which I had before examined; while from the opposite side of the stream, here much contracted, rose a perpendicular wall, I will not venture to say how many hundred feet, but only that it was the highest perpendicular wall of bare rock that I ever saw. In front of me tumbled in from the summit of the cliff a tributary stream, making a beautiful cascade, which was a remarkable fall in itself, and there was a cleft in this precipice, apparently four or five feet wide, perfectly straight up and down from top to bottom, which, from its cavernous depth and darkness, appeared merely as a *black streak*. This precipice is not sloped, nor is the material soft and crumbling slate as at Montmorenci, but it rises perfectly perpendicular, like the side of a mountain fortress, and is cracked into vast cubical masses of gray and black rock shining with moisture, as if it were the ruin of an ancient wall built by Titans. Birches, spruces, mountain-ashes with their bright red berries, arborvitaes, white pines, alders, &c., overhung this chasm on the very verge of the cliff and in the crevices, and here and there were buttresses of rock supporting trees part way down, yet so as to enhance, not injure, the effect of the bare rock. Take it altogether, it was a most wild and rugged and stupendous chasm, so deep and narrow where a river had worn itself a passage through a mountain of rock, and all around was the comparatively untrodden wilderness.

This was the limit of our walk down the St. Lawrence. Early in the afternoon we began to retrace our steps, not being able to cross the north channel and return by the Isle of Orleans, on account of the *trop grand vent,* or too great wind. Though the waves did run pretty high, it was evident that the inhabitants of Montmorenci County were no sailors, and made but little use of the river. When we reached the bridge, between St. Anne and Chateau Richer, I ran back a little way to ask a man in the field the name of the river which we were crossing, but for a long time I could not make out what he said, for he was one of the more unintelligible Jacques Cartier men. At last it flashed upon me that it was *La*

Rivière au Chien, or the Dog River, which my eyes beheld, which brought to my mind the life of the Canadian voyageur and *coureur de bois,* a more western and wilder Arcadia, methinks, than the world has ever seen; for the Greeks, with all their wood and river gods, were not so qualified to name the natural features of a country, as the ancestors of these French Canadians; and if any people had a right to substitute their own for the Indian names, it was they. They have preceded the pioneer on our own frontiers, and named the *prairie* for us. *La Rivière au Chien* cannot, by any license of language, be translated into Dog River, for that is not such a giving it to the dogs, and recognizing their place in creation as the French implies. One of the tributaries of the St. Anne is named *La Rivière de la Rose;* and farther east are, *La Rivière de la Blondelle,* and *La Rivière de la Friponne.* Their very *rivière* meanders more than our *river.*

Yet the impression which this country made on me was commonly different from this. To a traveller from the Old World, Canada East may appear like a new country, and its inhabitants like colonists, but to me, coming from New England, and being a very green traveller withal—notwithstanding what I have said about Hudson's Bay—it appeared as old as Normandy itself, and realized much that I had heard of Europe and the Middle Ages. Even the names of humble Canadian villages affected me as if they had been those of the renowned cities of antiquity. To be told by a habitan, when I asked the name of a village in sight, that it is *St. Fereole* or *St. Anne*, the *Guardian Angel* or the *Holy Joseph's;* or of a mountain, that it was *Bélange* or *St. Hyacinthe!* As soon as you leave the States, these saintly names begin. *St. John* is the first town you stop at (fortunately we did not see it), and thenceforward, the names of the mountains, and streams, and villages reel, if I may so speak, with the intoxication of poetry—*Chambly, Longueil, Pointe aux Trembles, Bartholomy*, &c., &c.; as if it needed only a little foreign accent, a few more liquids and vowels perchance in the language, to make us locate our ideals at once. I began to dream of Provence and the Troubadours, and of places and things which have no existence on the earth. They veiled the Indian and the primitive forest, and the woods toward Hudson's Bay, were only as the forests of France and Germany. I could not at once bring myself to believe that the inhabitants who pronounced daily those beautiful and, to me, significant names, lead as prosaic lives as we of New England. In short, the Canada which I saw was not merely a place for railroads to terminate in and for criminals to run to.

When I asked the man to whom I have referred, if there were any falls on the Rivière au Chien—for I saw that it came over the same high bank with the Montmorenci and St. Anne—he answered that there were. How far? I inquired. *Trois quatres lieue.* How high? *Je pense, quatre-vingt-dix pieds;* that is, ninety feet. We turned aside to look at the falls of the *Rivière du Sault à la Puce,* half a mile from the road, which before we had passed in our haste and ignorance, and we pronounced them as beautiful as any that we saw; yet they seemed to make no account of them there, and, when first we inquired the way to the Falls, directed us to Montmorenci, seven miles distant. It was evident that this was the country for waterfalls; that every stream that empties into the St. Lawrence, for some hundreds of miles, must have a great fall or cascade on it, and in its passage through the mountains was, for a short distance, a small Saguenay, with its upright walls. This fall of La Puce, the least remarkable of the four which we visited in this vicinity, we had never heard of till we came to Canada, and yet, so far as I know, there is nothing of the kind in New England to be compared with it.

Most travellers in Canada would not hear of it, though they might go so near as to hear it. Since my return I find that in the topographical description of the country mention is made of "two or three romantic falls" on this stream, though we saw and heard of but this one. Ask the inhabitants respecting any stream, if there is a fall on it, and they will perchance tell you of something as interesting as Bashpish or the Catskill, which no traveller has ever seen, or if they have not found it, you may possibly trace up the stream and discover it yourself. Falls there are a drug; and we became quite dissipated in respect to them. We had drank too much of them. Beside these which I have referred to, there are a thousand other falls on the St. Lawrence and its tributaries which I have not seen nor heard of; and above all there is one which I have heard of, called Niagara, so that I think that this river must be the most remarkable for its falls of any in the world.

At a house near the western boundary of Chateau Richer, whose master was said to speak a very little English, having recently lived at Quebec, we got lodging for the night. As usual, we had to go down a lane to get round to the south side of the house where the door was away from the road. For these Canadian houses have no front door, properly speaking. Every part is for the use of the occupant exclusively, and no part has reference to the traveller or to travel. Every New England house, on the contrary, has a front and principal door opening to the great world, though it may be on the cold side, for it stands on the highway of nations, and the road which runs by it comes from the Old World and goes to the far West; but the Canadian's door opens into his back-yard and farm alone, and the road which runs behind his house leads only from the church of one saint to that of another. We found a large family, hired men, wife and children, just eating their supper. They prepared some for us afterwards. The hired men were a merry crew of short, black-eyed fellows, and the wife a thin-faced, sharp-featured French Canadian woman. Our host's English staggered us rather more than any French we had heard yet; indeed, we found that even we spoke better French than he did English, and we concluded that a less crime would be committed on the whole if we spoke French with him, and in no respect aided or abetted his attempts to speak English. We had a long and merry chat with the family this Sunday evening in their spacious kitchen. While my companion smoked a pipe and parlez-vous'd with one party, I parleyed and gesticulated to another. The whole family was enlisted, and I kept a little girl writing what was otherwise unintelligible. The geography getting obscure, we called for chalk, and the greasy oiled table-cloth having been wiped—for it needed no French, but only a sentence from the universal language of looks on my part, to indicate that it needed it—we drew the St. Lawrence, with its parishes, thereon, and thenceforward went on swimmingly, by turns handling the chalk and committing to the table-cloth what would otherwise have been left in a limbo of unintelligibility. This was greatly to the entertainment of all parties. I was amused to hear how much use they made of the word *oui* in conversation with one another. After repeated single insertions of it, one would suddenly throw back his head at the same time with his chair, and exclaim rapidly, *"oui! oui! oui! oui!"* like a Yankee driving pigs. Our host told us that the farms thereabouts were generally two acres, or three hundred and sixty French feet wide, by one and a half leagues (?), or a little more than four and a half of our miles deep. This use of the word *acre* as long measure arises from the fact that the French acre or arpent, the arpent of Paris, makes a square of ten perches, of eighteen feet each on a side, a Paris foot being equal to 1.06575 English feet.

He said that the wood was cut off about one mile from the river. The rest was "bush," and beyond that the "Queen's bush." Old as the country is, each landholder bounds on the primitive forest, and fuel bears no price. As I had forgotten the French for *sickle,* they went out in the evening to the barn and got one, and so clenched the certainty of our understanding one another. Then, wishing to learn if they used the cradle, and not knowing any French word for this instrument, I set up the knives and forks on the blade of the sickle to represent one; at which they all exclaimed that they knew and had used it. When *snells* were mentioned they went out in the dark and plucked some. They were pretty good. They said they had three kinds of plums growing wild—blue, white, and red, the two former much alike and the best. Also they asked me if I would have *des pommes,* some apples, and got me some. They were exceedingly fair and glossy, and it was evident that there was no worm in them; but they were as hard almost as a stone, as if the season was too short to mellow them. We had seen no soft and yellow apples by the roadside. I declined eating one, much as I admired it, observing that it would be good *dans le printemps,* in the spring. In the morning when the mistress had set the eggs a-frying she nodded to a thickset, jolly-looking fellow, who rolled up his sleeves, seized the long-handled griddle, and commenced a series of revolutions and evolutions with it, ever and anon tossing its contents into the air, where they turned completely topsy-turvy and came down t' other side up; and this he repeated till they were done. That appeared to be his duty when eggs were concerned. I did not chance to witness this performance, but my companion did, and he pronounced it a master-piece in its way. This man's farm, with the buildings, cost seven hundred pounds; some smaller ones, two hundred.

In 1827, Montmorenci County, to which the Isle of Orleans has since been added, was nearly as large as Massachusetts, being the eighth county out of forty (in Lower Canada) in extent; but by far the greater part still must continue to be waste land, lying, as it were, under the walls of Quebec.

I quote these old statistics, not merely because of the difficulty of obtaining more recent ones, but also because I saw there so little evidence of any recent growth. There were in this county, at the same date, five Roman Catholic churches, and no others, five curés and five presbyteries, two schools, two corn-mills, four saw-mills, one carding-mill

—no medical man, or notary or lawyer—five shopkeepers, four taverns (we saw no sign of any, though, after a little hesitation, we were sometimes directed to some undistinguished hut as such), thirty artisans, and five river crafts, whose tonnage amounted to sixty-nine tons! This, notwithstanding that it has a frontage of more than thirty miles on the river, and the population is almost wholly confined to its banks. This describes nearly enough what we saw. But double some of these figures, which, however, its growth will not warrant, and you have described a poverty which not even its severity of climate and ruggedness of soil will suffice to account for. The principal productions were wheat, potatoes, oats, hay, peas, flax, maple-sugar, &c., &c.; linen, cloth, or *étoffe du pays*, flannel, and homespun, or *petite étoffe*.

In Lower Canada, according to Bouchette, there are two tenures—the feudal and the socage. Tenanciers, censitaires, or holders of land *en roture*, pay a small annual rent to the seigneurs, to which "is added some article of provision, such as a couple of fowls, or a goose, or a bushel of wheat." "They are also bound to grind their corn at the *moulin banal*, or the lord's mill, where one fourteenth part of it is taken for his use" as toll. He says that the toll is one twelfth in the

United States, where competition exists. It is not permitted to exceed one sixteenth in Massachusetts. But worse than this monopolizing of mill rents is what are called *lods et ventes,* or mutation fines. According to which the seigneur has "a right to a twelfth part of the purchase-money of every estate within his seigniory that changes its owner by sale." This is over and above the sum paid to the seller. In such cases, moreover, "the lord possesses the *droit de retrait,* which is the privilege of pre-emption at the highest bidden price within forty days after the sale has taken place"—a right which, however, is said to be seldom exercised. "Lands held by Roman Catholics are further subject to the payment to their curates of one twenty-sixth part of all the grain produced upon them, and to occasional assessments for building and repairing churches," &c.—a tax to which they are not subject if the proprietors change their faith; but they are not the less attached to their church in consequence. There are, however, various modifications of the feudal tenure. Under the socage tenure, which is that of the townships or more recent settlements, English, Irish, Scotch, and others, and generally of Canada West, the landholder is wholly unshackled by such conditions as I have quoted, and "is bound to no other obligations than those of allegiance to the king and obedience to the laws." Through-out Canada "a freehold of forty shillings yearly value, or the payment of ten pounds rent annually, is the qualification for voters." In 1846 more than one sixth of the whole population of Canada East were qualified to vote for members of Parliament—a greater proportion than enjoy a similar privilege in the United States.

The population which we had seen the last two days—I mean the habitans of Montmorenci County—appeared very inferior, intellectually and even physically, to that of New England. In some respects they were incredibly filthy. It was evident that they had not advanced since the settlement of the country, that they were quite behind the age, and fairly represented their ancestors in Normandy a thousand years ago. Even in respect to the common arts of life, they are not so far advanced as a frontier town in the West three years old. They have no money invested in railroad stock, and probably never will have. If they have got a French phrase for a railroad, it is as much as you can expect of them. They are very far from a revolution; have no quarrel with Church or State, but their vice and their virtue is content. As for annexation, they have never dreamed of it; indeed, they have not a clear idea what or where the States are. The English government has been remarkably liberal to its Catholic subjects in Canada, permitting them to wear their own fetters, both political and religious, as far as was possible for subjects. Their government is even too good for them. Parliament passed "an act [in 1825] to provide for the extinction of feudal and seigniorial rights and burdens on lands in Lower Canada, and for the gradual conversion of those tenures into the tenure of free and common socage," &c. But as late as 1831, at least, the design of the act was likely to be frustrated, owing to the reluctance of the seigniors and peasants. It has been observed by another that the French Canadians do not extend nor perpetuate their influence. The British, Irish, and other immigrants, who have settled the townships, are found to have imitated the American settlers, and not the French. They reminded me in this of the Indians, whom they were slow to displace and to whose habits of life they themselves more readily conformed than the Indians to theirs. The Governor-General Denouville remarked, in 1685, that some had long thought that it was necessary to bring the Indians near them in order to Frenchify (*franciser*) them, but that they had every reason to think themselves in an error; for those who had come near them and were even collected in villages in the midst of the colony had not become French, but the French, who had haunted them, had become savages. Kalm said: "Though many nations imitate the French customs, yet I observed, on the contrary, that the French in Canada, in many respects, follow the customs of the Indians, with whom they converse every day. They make use of the tobacco-pipes, shoes, garters, and girdles of the Indians. They follow the Indian way of making war with exactness; they mix the same things with tobacco (he might have said that both French and English learned the use itself of this weed of the Indian); they make use of the Indian bark-boats, and row them in the Indian way; they wrap square pieces of cloth round their feet instead of stockings; and have adopted many other Indian fashions." Thus, while the descendants of the Pilgrims are teaching the English to make pegged boots, the descendants of the French in Canada are wearing the Indian moccasin still. The French, to their credit be it said, to a certain extent respected the Indians as a separate and independent people, and spoke of them and contrasted themselves with them as the English have never done. They not only went to war with them as allies, but they lived at home with them as neighbors. In 1627 the French king declared "that the descendants of the French, settled in" New France, "and the savages who should be brought to the knowledge of the faith, and should make profession of it, should be counted and reputed French born *(Naturels François);* and as such could emigrate to France, when it seemed good to them, and there acquire, will, inherit, &c., &c., without obtaining letters of naturalization." When the English had possession of Quebec, in 1630, the Indians, attempting to practise the same familiarity with them that they had with the French, were driven out of their houses with blows; which accident taught them a difference between the two races, and attached them yet more to the French. The impression made on me was, that the French Canadians were even sharing the fate of the Indians, or at least gradually disappearing in what is called the Saxon current.

The English did not come to America from a mere love of adventure, nor to truck with or convert the savages, nor to hold offices under the crown, as the French to a great extent did, but to live in earnest and with freedom. The latter overran a great extent of country, selling strong water, and collecting its furs, and converting its inhabitants—or at least baptizing its dying infants *(enfants moribonds)*—without *improving* it. First, went the *coureur de bois* with the *eau de vie;* then followed, if he did not precede, the heroic missionary with the *eau d'immortalité.* It was freedom to hunt, and fish, and convert, not to work, that they sought. Hontan says that the *coureurs de bois* lived like sailors ashore. In no part of the seventeenth century could the French be said to have had a foothold in Canada; they held only by the fur of the wild animals which they were exterminating. To enable the poor seigneurs to get their living, it was permitted by a decree passed in the reign of Louis the Fourteenth, in 1685, "to all nobles and gentlemen settled in Canada, to engage in commerce, without being called to account or reputed to have done anything derogatory." The reader can infer to what extent they had engaged in agriculture, and how their farms must have shone by this time. The New England youth, on the other hand, were never *coureurs de bois* nor *voyageurs,* but backwoodsmen and sailors rather. Of all nations the English undoubtedly have proved hitherto that they had the most business here.

Yet I am not sure but I have most sympathy with that spirit of adventure which distinguished the French and Spaniards of those days, and made them especially the explorers of the American Continent—which so early carried the former to the Great Lakes and the Mississipi on the north, and the latter to the same river on the south. It was long before our frontiers reached their settlements in the West. So far as inland discovery was concerned, the adventurous spirit of the English was that of sailors who land but for a day, and their enterprise the enterprise of traders.

There was apparently a greater equality of condition among the habitans of Montmorenci County than in New England. They are an almost exclusively agricultural, and so far independent, population, each family producing nearly all the necessaries of life for itself. If the Canadian wants energy, perchance he possesses those virtues, social and others, which the Yankee lacks, in which case he cannot be regarded as a poor man.

IV

THE WALLS OF QUEBEC

After spending the night at a farm-house in Chateau-Richer, about a dozen miles northeast of Quebec, we set out on our return to the city. We stopped at the next house, a picturesque old stone mill, over the *Chipré*—for so the name sounded—such as you will nowhere see in the States, and asked the millers the age of the mill. They went up stairs to call the master; but the crabbed old miser asked why we wanted to know, and would tell us only for some compensation. I wanted French to give him a piece of my mind. I had got enough to talk on a pinch, but not to quarrel; so I had to come away, looking all I would have said.

This was the utmost incivility we met with in Canada. In Beauport, within a few miles of Quebec, we turned aside to look at a church which was just being completed—a very large and handsome edifice of stone, with a green bough stuck in its gable, of some significance to Catholics. The comparative wealth of the Church in this country was apparent; for in this village we did not see one good house besides. They were all humble cottages; and yet this appeared to me a more imposing structure than any church in Boston. But I am no judge of these things.

Re-entering Quebec through St. John's Gate, we took a caleche in Market Square for the Falls of the Chaudière, about nine miles southwest of the city, for which we were to pay so much, beside forty sous for tolls. The driver, as usual, spoke French only. The number of these vehicles is very great for so small a town. They are like one of our chaises that has lost its top, only stouter and longer in the body, with a seat for the driver where the dasher is with us, and broad leather ears on each side to protect the riders from the wheel and keep children from falling out. They had an easy jaunting look, which, as our hours were numbered, persuaded us to be riders. We met with them on every road near Quebec these days, each with its complement of two inquisitive-looking foreigners and a Canadian driver, the former evidently enjoying their novel experience, for commonly it is only the horse whose language you do not understand; but they were one remove further from him by the intervention of an equally unintelligible driver. We crossed the St. Lawrence to Point Levi in a French-Canadian ferry-boat, which was inconvenient and dirty, and managed with great noise and bustle. The current was very strong and tumultuous, and the boat tossed enough to make some sick, though it was only a mile across; yet the wind was not to be compared with that of the day before, and we saw that the Canadians had a good excuse for not taking us over to the Isle of Orleans in a pirogue, however shiftless they may be for not having provided any other conveyance. The route which we took to the Chaudière did not afford us those views of Quebec which we had expected, and the country and inhabitants appeared less interesting to a traveller than those we had seen. The Falls of the Chaudière are three miles from its mouth on the south side of the St. Lawrence. Though they were the largest which I saw in Canada, I was not proportionately interested by them, probably from satiety. I did not

see any *peculiar* propriety in the name *Chaudière,* or cal-
dron. I saw here the most brilliant rainbow that I ever imagined. It was just across the stream below the precipice,
formed on the mist which this tremendous fall produced;
and I stood on a level with the key-stone of its arch. It was
not a few faint prismatic colors merely, but a full semi-circle,
only four or five rods in diameter, though as wide as usual,
so intensely bright as to pain the eye, and apparently as substantial as an arch of stone. It changed its position and colors
as we moved, and was the brighter because the sun shone so
clearly and the mist was so thick. Evidently a picture painted
on mist for the men and animals that came to the falls to
look at; but for what special purpose beyond this, I know not.
At the farthest point in this ride, and when most inland,
unexpectedly at a turn in the road we descried the frowning
citadel of Quebec in the horizon, like the beak of a bird of
prey. We returned by the river-road under the bank, which is
very high, abrupt, and rocky. When we were opposite to
Quebec, I was surprised to see that in the Lower Town, under
the shadow of the rock, the lamps were lit, twinkling not
unlike crystals in a cavern, while the citadel high above, and
we, too, on the south shore, were in broad daylight. As we

were too late for the ferry-boat that night, we put up at a *maison de pension* at Point Levi. The usual two-story stove was here placed against an opening in the partition shaped like a fireplace, and so warmed several rooms. We could not understand their French here very well, but the *potage* was just like what we had had before. There were many small chambers with door-ways but no doors. The walls of our chamber, all around and overhead, were neatly ceiled, and the timbers cased with wood unpainted. The pillows were checkered and tasselled, and the usual long-pointed red woollen or worsted night-cap was placed on each. I pulled mine out to see how it was made. It was in the form of a double cone, one end tucked into the other; just such, it appeared, as I saw men wearing all day in the streets. Probably I should have put it on if the cold had been then, as it is sometimes there, thirty or forty degrees below zero.

When we landed at Quebec the next morning, a man lay on his back on the wharf, apparently dying, in the midst of a crowd and directly in the path of the horses, groaning, "*O ma conscience!*" I thought that he pronounced his French more distinctly than any I heard, as if the dying had already acquired the accents of a universal language. Having secured the only unengaged berths in the Lord Sydenham steamer, which was to leave Quebec before sundown, and being resolved, now that I had seen somewhat of the country, to get an idea of the city, I proceeded to walk round the Upper Town, or fortified portion, which is two miles and three quarters in circuit, alone, as near as I could get to the cliff and the walls, like a rat looking for a hole; going round by the southwest, where there is but a single street between the cliff and the water, and up the long, wooden stairs, through the suburbs northward to the King's Woodyard, which I thought must have been a long way from his fireplace, and under the cliffs of the St. Charles, where the drains issue under the walls, and the walls are loop-holed for musketry; so returning by Mountain Street and Prescott Gate to the Upper Town. Having found my way by an obscure passage near the St. Louis Gate to the glacis on the north of the citadel proper—I believe that I was the only visitor then in the city who got in there—I enjoyed a prospect nearly as good as from within the citadel itself, which I had explored some days before. As I walked on the glacis I heard the sound of a bagpipe from the soldiers' dwellings in the rock, and was further soothed and affected by the sight of a soldier's cat walking up a cleated plank into a high loophole, designed for *mus-catry*, as serene as Wisdom herself, and with a gracefully waving motion of her tail, as if her ways were ways of pleasantness and all her paths were peace. Scaling a slat fence, where a small force might have checked me, I got out of the esplanade into the Governor's Garden, and read the well-known inscription on Wolfe and Montcalm's monument, which for saying much in little, and that to the purpose, undoubtedly deserved the prize medal which it received:

MORTEM. VIRTUS. COMMUNEM.
FAMAM. HISTORIA.
MONUMENTUM. POSTERITAS.
DEDIT.

Valor gave them one death, history one fame, posterity one monument. The Government Garden has for nosegays, amid kitchen vegetables, beside the common garden flowers, the usual complement of cannon directed toward some future and possible enemy. I then returned up St. Louis Street to the esplanade and ramparts there, and went round the Upper

Town once more, though I was very tired, this time on the *inside* of the wall; for I knew that the wall was the main thing in Quebec and had cost a great deal of money, and therefore I must make the most of it. In fact, these are the only remarkable walls we have in North America, though we have a good deal of Virginia fence, it is true. Moreover, I cannot say but I yielded in some measure to the soldier instinct, and, having but a short time to spare, thought it best to examine the wall thoroughly, that I might be the better prepared if I should ever be called that way again in the service of my country. I committed all the gates to memory in their order, which did not cost me so much trouble as it would have done at the hundred-gated city, there being only five; nor were they so hard to remember, as those seven of Boeotian Thebes; and, moreover, I thought that, if seven champions were enough against the latter, one would be enough against Quebec, though he bore for all armor and device only an umbrella and a bundle. I took the nunneries as I went, for I had learned to distinguish them by the blinds; and I observed also the foundling hospitals and the convents, and whatever was attached to, or in the vicinity of the walls. All the rest I omitted, as naturally as one would the inside of an inedible shellfish. These were the only pearls, and the wall the only mother-of-pearl for me. Quebec is chiefly famous for the thickness of its parietal bones. The technical terms of its conchology may stagger a beginner a little at first, such as *banlieue, esplanade, glacis, ravelin, cavalier,* &c., &c., but with the aid of a comprehensive dictionary you soon learn the nature of your ground. I was surprised at the extent of the artillery barracks, built so long ago—*Casernes Nouvelles,* they used to be called—nearly six hundred feet in length by forty in depth, where the sentries, like peripatetic philosophers, were so absorbed in thought, as not to notice me when I passed in and out at the gates. Within, are "small arms of every description, sufficient for the equipment of twenty thousand men," so arranged as to give a startling *coup d'oeil* to strangers. I did not enter, not wishing to get a black eye; for they are said to be "in a state of complete repair and readiness for immediate use." Here, for a short time, I lost sight of the wall, but I recovered it again on emerging from the barrack yard. There I met with a Scotchman who appeared to have business with the wall, like myself; and, being thus mutually drawn together by a similarity of tastes, we had a little conversation *sub moenibus,* that is, by an angle of the

wall which sheltered us. He lived about thirty miles northwest of Quebec; had been nineteen years in the country; said
he was disappointed that he was not brought to America after
all, but found himself still under British rule and where his
own language was not spoken; that many Scotch, Irish, and
English were disappointed in like manner, and either went to
the States, or pushed up the river to Canada West, nearer to
the States, and where their language was spoken. He talked of
visiting the States some time; and, as he seemed ignorant of
geography, I warned him that it was one thing to visit the
State of Massachusetts, and another to visit the State of California. He said it was colder there than usual at that season,
and he was lucky to have brought his thick togue, or frock-
coat, with him; thought it would snow, and then be pleasant
and warm. That is the way we are always thinking. However,
his words were music to me in my thin hat and sack.

At the ramparts on the cliff near the old Parliament
House I counted twenty-four thirty-two-pounders in a row,
pointed over the harbor, with their balls piled pyramid-wise
between them—there are said to be in all about one hundred
and eighty guns mounted at Quebec—all which were faith-
fully kept dusted by officials, in accordance with the motto,

"In time of peace prepare for war"; but I saw no preparations for peace: she was plainly an uninvited guest.

Having thus completed the circuit of this fortress, both within and without, I went no farther by the wall for fear that I should become wall-eyed. However, I think that I deserve to be made a member of the Royal Sappers and Miners.

In short, I observed everywhere the most perfect arrangements for keeping a wall in order, not even permitting the lichens to grow on it, which some think an ornament; but then I saw no cultivation nor pasturing within it to pay for the outlay, and cattle were strictly forbidden to feed on the glacis under the severest penalties. Where the dogs get their milk I don't know, and I fear it is bloody at best.

The citadel of Quebec says, "I *will* live here, and you sha'n't prevent me." To which you return, that you have not the slightest objection; live and let live. The Martello towers looked, for all the world, exactly like abandoned wind-mills which had not had a grist to grind these hundred years. Indeed, the whole castle here was a "folly"—England's folly—and, in more senses than one, a castle in the air. The inhabitants and the government are gradually waking up to a sense of this truth; for I heard something said about their abandoning the wall around the Upper Town, and confining the fortifications to the citadel of forty acres. Of course they will finally reduce their intrenchments to the circumference of their own brave hearts.

The most modern fortifications have an air of antiquity about them; they have the aspect of ruins in better or worse repair from the day they are built, because they are not really the work of this age. The very place where the soldier resides has a peculiar tendency to become old and dilapidated, as the word *barrack* implies. I couple all fortifications in my mind with the dismantled Spanish forts to be found in so many parts of the world; and if in any place they are not actually dismantled, it is because that there the intellect of the inhabitants is dismantled. The commanding officer of an old fort near Valdivia in South America, when a traveller remarked to him that, with one discharge, his gun-carriages would certainly fall to pieces, gravely replied, "No, I am sure, sir, they would stand two." Perhaps the guns of Quebec would stand three. Such structures carry us back to the Middle Ages, the siege of Jerusalem, and St. Jean d'Acre, and the days of the Bucaniers. In the armory of the citadel they showed me a clumsy implement, long since useless, which they called a Lombard gun. I thought that their whole citadel was such a Lombard gun, fit object for the museums of the curious. Such works do not consist with the development of the intellect. Huge stone structures of all kinds, both in their erection and by their influence when erected, rather oppress than liberate the mind. They are tombs for the souls of men, as frequently for their bodies also. The sentinel with his musket beside a man with his umbrella is spectral. There is not sufficient reason for his existence. Does my friend there, with a bullet resting on half an ounce of powder, think that he needs that argument in conversing with me? The fort was the first institution that was founded here, and it is amusing to read in Champlain how assiduously they worked at it almost from the first day of the settlement. The founders of the colony thought this an excellent site for a wall—and no doubt it was a better site, in some respects, for a wall than for a city—but it chanced that a city got behind it. It chanced, too, that a Lower Town got before it, and clung like an oyster to the outside of the crags, as you may see at low tide. It is as if you were to come to a country village surrounded by palisades in the old Indian fashion—interesting only as a relic of antiquity and barbarism. A fortified town is like a man cased in the heavy armor of antiquity, with a horse-load of broad-swords and small arms slung to him, endeavoring to go about his business. Or is this an indispensable machinery for the good government of the country? The inhabitants of California succeed pretty well, and are doing better and better every day, without any such institution. What use has this fortress served, to look at it even from the soldiers' point of view? At first the French took care of it; yet Wolfe sailed by it with impunity, and took the town of Quebec without experiencing any hindrance at last from its fortifications. They were only the bone for which the parties fought. Then the English began to take care of it. So of any fort in the world—that in Boston harbor, for instance. We shall at length hear that an enemy sailed by it in the night, for it cannot sail itself, and both it and its inhabitants are always benighted. How often we read that the enemy occupied a position which commanded the old, and so the fort was evacuated. Have not the school-house and the printing-press occupied a position which commands such a fort as this?

However, this is a ruin kept in remarkably good repair. There are some eight hundred or thousand men there to exhibit it. One regiment goes bare-legged to increase the attraction. If you wish to study the muscles of the leg about the knee, repair to Quebec. This universal exhibition in Canada of the tools and sinews of war reminded me of the keeper of a menagerie showing his animals' claws. It was the English leopard showing his claws. Always the *royal* something or other; as, at the menagerie, the Royal Bengal Tiger. Silliman states that "the cold is so intense in the winter nights, particularly on Cape Diamond, that the sentinels cannot stand it more than one hour, and are relieved at the expiration of that time"; "and even, as it is said, at much shorter intervals, in case of the most extreme cold." What a natural or unnatural fool must that soldier be—to say nothing of his government—who, when quicksilver is freezing and blood is ceasing to be quick, will stand to have his face frozen, watching the walls of Quebec, though, so far as they are concerned, both honest and dishonest men all the world over have been in their beds nearly half a century—or at least for that space travellers have visited Quebec only as they would read history. I shall never again wake up in a colder night than usual, but I shall think how rapidly the sentinels are relieving one another on the walls of Quebec, their quicksilver being all frozen, as if apprehensive that some hostile Wolfe may even then be scaling the Heights of Abraham, or some persevering Arnold about to issue from the wilderness; some Malay or Japanese, perchance, coming round by the northwest coast, have chosen that moment to assault the citadel! Why I should as soon expect to find the sentinels still relieving one another on the walls of Nineveh, which have so long been buried to the world! What a troublesome thing a wall is! I thought it was to defend me, and not I it. Of course, if they had no wall they would not need to have any sentinels.

You might venture to advertise this farm as well fenced with substantial stone walls (saying nothing about the eight hundred Highlanders and Royal Irish who are required to keep them from toppling down); stock and tools to go with the land if desired. But it would not be wise for the seller to exhibit his farmbook.

Why should Canada, wild and unsettled as it is, impress us as an older country than the States, unless because her institutions are old? All things appeared to contend there, as I have implied, with a certain rust of antiquity—such as forms on old armor and iron guns—the rust of conventions and formalities. It is said that the metallic roofs of Montreal and Quebec keep sound and bright for forty years in some cases. But if the rust was not on the tinned roofs and spires, it was on the inhabitants and their institutions. Yet the work of burnishing goes briskly forward. I imagined that the government vessels at the wharves were laden with rotten-stone and oxalic acid—that is what the first ship from England in the spring comes freighted with—and the hands of the colonial legislature are cased in washleather. The principal exports must be *gunny* bags, verdigrease, and iron rust. Those who first built this fort, coming from Old France with the memory and tradition of feudal days and customs weighing on them, were unquestionably behind their age; and those who now inhabit and repair it are behind their ancestors or predecessors. Those old chevaliers thought that they could transplant the feudal system to America. It has been set out, but it has not thriven. Notwithstanding that Canada was settled first, and, unlike New England, for a long series of years enjoyed the fostering care of the mother country—notwithstanding that, as Charlevoix tells us, it had more of the ancient *noblesse* among its early settlers than any other of the French colonies, and perhaps than all the others together—there are in both the Canadas but 600,000 of

French descent to-day—about half so many as the population of Massachusetts. The whole population of both Canadas is but about 1,700,000 Canadians, English, Irish, Scotch, Indians, and all, put together! Samuel Laing, in his essay on the Northmen, to whom especially, rather than the Saxons, he refers the energy and indeed the excellence of the English character, observes that, when they occupied Scandinavia, "each man possessed his lot of land without reference to, or acknowledgment of, any other man—without any local chief to whom his military service or other quit-rent for his land was due—without tenure from, or duty or obligation to, any superior, real or fictitious, except the general sovereign. The individual settler held his land, as his descendants in Norway still express it, by the same right as the king held his crown—by udal right, or adel—that is, noble right." The French have occupied Canada, not *udally*, or by noble right, but *feudally*, or by ignoble right. They are a nation of peasants.

It was evident that, both on account of the feudal system and the aristocratic government, a private man was not worth so much in Canada as in the United States; and, if your wealth in any measure consists in manliness, in originality, and independence, you had better stay here. How could a peaceable, freethinking man live neighbor to the Forty-ninth Regiment? A New-Englander would naturally be a bad citizen, probably a rebel, there—certainly if he were already a rebel at home. I suspect that a poor man who is not servile is a much rarer phenomenon there and in England than in the Northern United States. An Englishman, methinks—not to speak of other European nations— habitually regards himself merely as a constituent part of the English nation; he is a member of the royal regiment of Englishmen, and is proud of his company, as he has reason to be proud of it. But an American—one who has made a tolerable use of his opportunities—cares, comparatively, little about such things, and is advantageously nearer to the primitive and the ultimate condition of man in these respects. It is a government, that English one—like most other European ones—that cannot afford to be forgotten, as you would naturally forget it; under which one cannot be wholesomely neglected, and grow up a man and not an Englishman merely—cannot be a poet even without danger of being made poet-laureate! Give me a country where it is the most natural thing in the world for a government that does not understand you to let you alone. One would say that a true

Englishman could speculate only within bounds. (It is true the Americans have proved that they, in more than one sense, can *speculate* without bounds.) He has to pay his respects to so many things, that, before he knows it, he *may* have paid away all he is worth. What makes the United States government, on the whole, more tolerable—I mean for us lucky white men—is the fact that there is so much less of government with us. Here it is only once in a month or a year that a man *needs* remember that institution; and those who go to Congress can play the game of the Kilkenny cats there without fatal consequences to those who stay at home—their term is so short: but in Canada you are reminded of the government every day. It parades itself before you. It is not content to be the servant, but will be the master; and every day it goes out to the Plains of Abraham or to the Champ de Mars and exhibits itself and its tools. Everywhere there appeared an attempt to make and to preserve trivial and otherwise transient distinctions. In the streets of Montreal and Quebec you met not only with soldiers in red, and shuffling priests in unmistakable black and white, with Sisters of Charity gone into mourning for their deceased relative—not to mention the nuns of various orders depending on the fashion of a tear, of whom you heard—but youths belonging to some seminary or other, wearing coats edged with white, who looked as if their expanding hearts were already repressed with a piece of tape. In short, the inhabitants of Canada appeared to be suffering between two fires—the soldiery and the priesthood.

V

THE SCENERY OF QUEBEC;
AND THE RIVER ST. LAWRENCE

About twelve o'clock this day, being in the Lower Town, I looked up at the signal-gun by the flagstaff on Cape Diamond, and saw a soldier up in the heavens there making preparations to fire it—both he and the gun in bold relief against the sky. Soon after, being warned by the boom of the gun to look up again, there was only the cannon in the sky, the smoke just blowing away from it, as if the soldier, having touched it off, and concealed himself for effect, leaving the sound to echo grandly from shore to shore, and far up and down the river. This answered the purpose of a dinner-horn.

There are no such restaurateurs in Quebec or Montreal as there are in Boston. I hunted an hour or two in vain in this town to find one, till I lost my appetite. In one house, called a restaurateur, where lunches were advertised, I found only tables covered with bottles and glasses innumerable, containing apparently a sample of every liquid that has been known since the earth dried up after the flood, but no scent of solid food did I perceive gross enough to excite a hungry mouse. In short, I saw nothing to tempt me there, but a large map of Canada against the wall. In another place I once more got as far as the bottles, and then asked for a bill of fare; was told to walk up stairs; had no bill of fare, nothing but fare. "Have you any pies or puddings?" I inquired, for I am obliged to keep my savageness in check by a low diet. "No, sir; we've nice mutton-chop, roast beef, beef-steak, cutlets," and so on. A burly Englishman, who was in the midst of the siege of a piece of roast beef and of whom I have never had a front view to this day, turned half round, with his mouth half full, and remarked, "You'll find no pies nor puddings in Quebec, sir; they don't make any here." I found that it was even so, and therefore bought some musty cake and some fruit in the open market-place. This marketplace by the water-side, where the old women sat by their tables in the open air, amid a dense crowd jabbering all languages, was the best place in Quebec to observe the people; and the ferry-boats, continually coming and going with their motley crews and cargoes, added much to the entertainment. I also saw them getting water from the river, for Quebec is supplied with water by cart and barrel. This city impressed me as wholly foreign and French, for I scarcely heard the sound of the English language in the streets. More than three fifths of the inhabitants are of French origin; and if the traveller did not visit the fortifications particularly, he might not be reminded that the English have any foothold here; and, in any case, if he looked no farther than Quebec, they would appear to have planted themselves in Canada only as they have in Spain at Gibraltar; and he who plants upon a rock cannot expect much increase. The novel sights and sounds by the water-side made me think of such ports as Boulogne, Dieppe, Rouen, and Havre de Grace, which I have never seen; but I have no doubt that they present similar scenes. I was much amused from first to last with the sounds made by the charette and caleche drivers. It was that part of their foreign language that you heard the most of—the French they talked to their horses—and which they talked the loudest. It was a more novel sound to me than the French of conversation. The streets resounded with the cries, *"Qui donc!" "March tôt!"* I suspect that many of our horses which came from Canada would prick up their ears at these sounds. Of the shops, I was most attracted by those where furs and Indian works were sold, as containing articles of genuine Canadian manufacture. I have been told that two townsmen of mine, who were interested in horticulture, travelling once in Canada, and being in Quebec, thought it would be a good opportunity to obtain seeds of the real Canada crook-neck squash. So they went into a shop where such things were advertised, and inquired for the same. The shopkeeper had the very thing they wanted. "But are you sure," they asked, "that these are the genuine Canada crook-neck?" "O yes, gentlemen," answered he, "they are a lot which I have received directly from Boston." I resolved that my Canada crook-neck seeds should be such as had grown in Canada.

Too much has not been said about the scenery of Quebec. The fortifications of Cape Diamond are omnipresent. They preside, they frown over the river and surrounding country. You travel ten, twenty, thirty miles up or down the river's banks, you ramble fifteen miles amid the hills on either

side, and then, when you have long since forgotten them, perchance slept on them by the way, at a turn of the road or of
your body, there they are still, with their geometry against
the sky. The child that is born and brought up thirty miles
distant, and has never travelled to the city, reads his country's
history, sees the level lines of the citadel amid the cloud-built
citadels in the western horizon, and is told that that is
Quebec. No wonder if Jacques Cartier's pilot exclaimed in
Norman French, *Que bec!*—"What a beak!"—when he saw
this cape, as some suppose. Every modern traveller involun-
tarily uses a similar expression. Particularly it is said that its
sudden apparition on turning Point Levi makes a memorable
impression on him who arrives by water. The view from Cape
Diamond has been compared by European travellers with the
most remarkable views of a similar kind in Europe, such as
from Edinburgh Castle, Gibraltar, Cintra, and others, and
preferred by many. A main peculiarity in this, compared with
other views which I have beheld, is that it is from the ramparts of a fortified city, and not from a solitary and majestic
river cape alone that this view is obtained. I associate the
beauty of Quebec with the steel-like and flashing air, which
may be peculiar to that season of the year, in which the blue

flowers of the succory and some late golden-rods and butter-cups on the summit of Cape Diamond were almost my only companions—the former bluer than the heavens they faced. Yet even I yielded in some degree to the influence of historical associations, and found it hard to attend to the geology of Cape Diamond or the botany of the Plains of Abraham. I still remember the harbor far beneath me, sparkling like silver in the sun—the answering highlands of Point Levi on the south-east—the frowning Cap Tourmente abruptly bounding the seaward view in the northeast—the villages of Lorette and Charlesbourg on the north—and further west the distant Val Cartier, sparkling with white cottages, hardly removed by distance through the clear air—not to mention a few blue mountains along the horizon in that direction. You look out from the ramparts of the citadel beyond the frontiers of civi-lization. Yonder small group of hills, according to the guide-book, forms "the portal of the wilds which are trodden only by the feet of the Indian hunters as far as Hudson's Bay." It is but a few years since Bouchette declared that the country ten leagues north of the British capital of North America was as little known as the middle of Africa. Thus the citadel under my feet, and all historical associations, were swept away again by an influence from the wilds and from nature, as if the beholder had read her history—an influence which, like the Great River itself, flowed from the Arctic fastnesses and Western forests with irresistible tide over all.

The most interesting object in Canada to me was the River St. Lawrence, known far and wide, and for centuries, as the Great River. Cartier, its discoverer, sailed up it as far as Montreal in 1535—nearly a century before the coming of the Pilgrims; and I have seen a pretty accurate map of it so far, containing the city of "Hochelaga" and the river "Saguenay," in Ortelius's *Theatrum Orbis Terrarum,* printed at Antwerp in 1575—the first edition having appeared in 1570—in which the famous cities of "Norumbega" and "Orsinora" stand on the rough-blocked continent where New England is to-day, and the fabulous but unfortunate Isle of Demons, and Frislant, and others, lie off and on in the unfrequented sea, some of them prowling near what is now the course of the Cunard steamers. In this ponderous folio of the "Ptolemy of his age," said to be the first general atlas published after the revival of the sciences in Europe, only one page of which is devoted to the topography of the *Novus Orbis,* the St. Lawrence is the only large river, whether drawn from fancy or from observation, on the east side of North America. It was famous in Europe before the other rivers of North America were heard of, notwithstanding that the mouth of the Mississippi is said to have been discovered first, and its stream was reached by Soto not long after; but the St. Lawrence had attracted settlers to its cold shores long before the Mississippi, or even the Hudson, was known to the world. Schoolcraft was misled by Gallatin into saying that Narvaez discovered the Mississippi. De Vega does *not* say so. The first explorers declared that the summer in that country was as warm as France, and they named one of the bays in the Gulf of St. Lawrence the Bay of Chaleur, or of warmth; but they said nothing about the winter being as cold as Greenland. In the manuscript account of Cartier's second voyage, attributed by some to that navigator himself, it is called "the greatest river, without comparison, that is known to have ever been seen." The savages told him that it was the *"chemin du Canada"*— the highway to Canada—"which goes so far that no man had ever been to the end that they had heard." The Saguenay, one of its tributaries, which the panorama has made known to New England within three years, is described by Cartier, in 1535, and still more particularly by Jean Alphonse, in 1542, who adds, "I think that this river comes from the sea of Cathay, for in this place there issues a strong current, and there runs there a terrible tide." The early explorers saw many whales and other sea-monsters far up the St. Lawrence. Champlain, in his map, represents a whale spouting in the harbor of Quebec, three hundred and sixty miles from what is called the mouth of the river; and Charlevoix takes his reader to the summit of Cape Diamond to see the "porpoises, white as snow," sporting on the surface of the harbor of Quebec. And Boucher says in 1664, "from there (Tadoussac) to Montreal is found a great quantity of *Marsouins blancs.*" Several whales have been taken pretty high up the river since I was there. P. A. Gosse, in his "Canadian Naturalist," p. 171 (London, 1840), speaks of "the white dolphin of the St. Lawrence *(Delphinus Canadensis),*" as considered different from those of the sea. "The Natural History Society of Montreal offered a prize, a few years ago, for an essay on the *Cetacea* of the St. Lawrence, which was, I believe, handed in." In Champlain's day it was commonly called "the Great River of Canada." More than one nation has claimed it. In Ogilby's "America of 1670," in the map *Novi Belgii,* it is called "De Groote Rivier van Niew Nederlandt." It bears different names in different parts of its course, as it flows through what were formerly the territories of different nations. From the Gulf to Lake Ontario it is called at present the St. Lawrence; from Montreal to the same place it is frequently called the Cateraqui; and higher up it is known successively as the Niagara, Detroit, St. Clair, St. Mary's, and St. Louis rivers. Humboldt, speaking of the Orinoco, says that this name is unknown in the interior of the country; so likewise the tribes that dwell about the sources of the St. Lawrence have never heard the name which it bears in the lower part of its course. It rises near another father of waters—the Mississippi—issuing from a remarkable spring far up in the woods, called Lake Superior, fifteen hundred miles in circumference; and several other springs there are thereabouts which feed it. It makes such a noise in its tumbling down at one place as is heard all round the world. Bouchette, the Surveyor-General of the Canadas, calls it "the most splendid river on the globe"; says that it is two thousand statute miles long (more recent geographers make it four or five hundred miles longer); that at the Rivière du Sud it is eleven miles wide; at the Traverse, thirteen; at the Paps of Matane, twenty-five; at the Seven Islands, seventy-three; and at its mouth, from Cape Rosier to the Mingan Settlements in Labrador, near one hundred and five (?) miles wide. According to Captain Bayfield's recent chart it is about *ninety-six* geographical miles wide at the latter place, measuring at right angles with the stream. It has much the largest estuary, regarding both length and breadth, of any river on the globe. Humboldt says that the river Plate, which has the broadest estuary of the South American rivers, is ninety-two geographical miles wide at its mouth; also he found the Orinoco to be more than three miles wide at five hundred and sixty miles from its mouth; but he does not tell us that ships of six hundred tons can sail up it so far, as they can up the St. Lawrence to Montreal—an equal distance. If he had described a fleet of such ships at anchor in a city's port so far inland, we should have got a very different idea of the Orinoco. Perhaps Charlevoix describes the St. Lawrence truly as the most *navigable* river in the world. Between Montreal and Quebec it averages about two miles wide. The tide is felt as far up as Three Rivers, four hundred and thirty-two miles, which is as far as from Boston to Washington. As far up as Cap aux Oyes, sixty or seventy miles below Quebec, Kalm found a great part of the plants near the shore to be marine, as glass-wort *(Salicornia)*, seaside pease *(Pisum maritimum)*, sea-milkwort *(Glaux)*, beach-grass *(Psamma arenarium)*, sea-side plantain *(Plantago maritima)*, the sea-rocket *(Bunias cakile)*, &c.

The geographer Guyot observes that the Maranon is three thousand miles long, and gathers its waters from a surface of a million and a half square miles; that the Mississippi is also three thousand miles long, but its basin covers only from eight to nine hundred thousand square miles; that the St. Lawrence is eighteen hundred miles long, and its basin covers more than a million square miles (Darby says five hundred thousand); and speaking of the lakes, he adds, "These vast fresh-water seas, together with the St. Lawrence, cover a surface of nearly one hundred thousand square miles, and it has been calculated that they contain about one half of all the fresh water on the surface of our planet." But all these calculations are necessarily very rude and inaccurate. Its tributaries, the Ottawa, St. Maurice, and Saguenay, are great rivers themselves. The latter is said to be more than one thousand (?) feet deep at its mouth, while its cliffs rise perpendicularly an equal distance above its surface. Pilots say there are no soundings till one hundred and fifty miles up the St. Lawrence. The greatest sounding in the river, given on

Bayfield's chart of the gulf and river, is two hundred and twenty-eight fathoms. McTaggart, an engineer, observes that "the Ottawa is larger than all the rivers in Great Britain, were they running in one." The traveller Grey writes: "A dozen Danubes, Rhines, Taguses, and Thameses would be nothing to twenty miles of fresh water in breadth (as where he happened to be), from ten to forty fathoms in depth." And again: "There is not perhaps in the whole extent of this immense continent so fine an approach to it as by the river St. Lawrence. In the Southern States you have, in general, a level country for many miles inland; here you are introduced at once into a majestic scenery, where everything is on a grand scale—mountains, woods, lakes, rivers, precipices, waterfalls."

We have not yet the data for a minute comparison of the St. Lawrence with the South American rivers; but it is obvious that, taking it in connection with its lakes, its estuary, and its falls, it easily bears off the palm from all the rivers on the globe; for though, as Bouchette observes, it may not carry to the ocean a greater volume of water than the Amazon and Mississippi, its surface and cubic mass are far greater than theirs. But, unfortunately, this noble river is closed by ice from the beginning of December to the middle of April. The arrival of the first vessel from England when the ice breaks up is, therefore, a great event, as when the salmon, shad, and ale-wives come up a river in the spring to relieve the famishing inhabitants on its banks. Who can say what would have been the history of this continent if, as has been suggested, this river had emptied into the sea where New York stands!

After visiting the Museum and taking one more look at the wall, I made haste to the Lord Sydenham steamer, which at five o'clock was to leave for Montreal. I had already taken a seat on deck, but finding that I had still an hour and a half to spare, and remembering that large map of Canada which I had seen in the parlor of the restaurateur in my search after pudding and realizing that I might never see the like out of the country, I returned thither, asked liberty to look at the map, rolled up the mahogany table, put my handkerchief on it, stood on it, and copied all I wanted before the maid came in and said to me standing on the table, "Some gentlemen want the room, sir"; and I retreated without having broken the neck of a single bottle, or my own, very thankful and willing to pay for all the solid food I had got. We were soon abreast of Cap Rouge, eight miles above Quebec, after we got underway. It was in this place, then called *"Fort du France Roy,"* that the Sieur de Roberval with his company, having sent home two of his three ships, spent the winter of 1542–43. It appears that they fared in the following manner (I translate from the original): "Each mess had only two loaves, weighing each a pound, and half a pound of beef. They ate pork for dinner, with half a pound of butter, and beef for supper, with about two handfuls of beans, without butter. Wednesdays, Fridays, and Saturdays they ate salted cod, and sometimes green, for dinner, with butter; and porpoise and beans for supper. Monsieur Roberval administered good justice, and punished each according to his offence. One named Michel Gaillon, was hung for theft; John of Nantes was put in irons and imprisoned for his fault; and others were likewise put in irons; and many were whipped, both men and women; by which means they lived in peace and tranquillity." In an account of a voyage up this river, printed in the Jesuit Relations in the year 1664, it is said: "It was an interesting navigation for us in ascending the river from Cap Tourment to Quebec, to see on this side and on that, for the space of eight leagues, the farms and the houses of the company, built by our French, all along these shores. On the right, the seigniories of Beauport, of Notre Dames des Anges; and on the left, this beautiful Isle of Orleans." The same traveller names among the fruits of the country observed at the Isles of Richelieu, at the head of Lake St. Peter, "kinds *(des espèces)* of little apples or haws *(semelles)*, and of pears, which only ripen with the frost."

Night came on before we had passed the high banks. We had come from Montreal to Quebec in one night. The return voyage, against the stream, takes about an hour longer. Jacques Cartier, the first white man who is known to have ascended this river, thus speaks of his voyage from what is now Quebec to the foot of Lake St. Peter, or about half-way to Montreal: "From the said day, the 19th, even to the 28th of the said month [September, 1535], we had been navigating up the said river without losing hour or day, during which time we had seen and found as much country and lands as level as we could desire, full of the most beautiful trees in the world," which he goes on to describe. But we merely slept and woke again to find that we had passed through all the country which he was eight days in sailing through. He must have had a troubled sleep. We were not long enough on the river to realize that it had length; we got only the impression of its breadth, as if we had passed over a lake a mile or two in breadth and several miles long, though we might thus have slept through a European kingdom. Being at the head of Lake St. Peter, on the above-mentioned 28th of September, dealing with the natives, Cartier says: "We inquired of them by signs if this was the route to Hochelaga [Montreal]; and they answered that it was, and that there were yet three day's journeys to go there." He finally arrived at Hochelaga on the 2d of October.

When I went on deck at dawn we had already passed through Lake St. Peter, and saw islands ahead of us. Our boat advancing with a strong and steady pulse over the calm surface, we felt as if we were permitted to be awake in the scenery of a dream. Many vivacious Lombardy poplars along the distant shores gave them a novel and lively, though artificial look, and contrasted strangely with the slender and graceful elms on both shores and islands. The church of Varennes, fifteen miles from Montreal, was conspicuous at a great distance before us, appearing to belong to, and rise out of, the river; and now, and before, Mount Royal indicated where the city was. We arrived about seven o'clock, and set forth immediately to ascend the mountain, two miles distant, going across lots in spite of numerous signs threatening the severest penalties to trespassers, past an old building known as the Mac Tavish property—Simon Mac Tavish, I suppose, whom Silliman refers to as "in a sense the founder of the North-western Company." His tomb was behind in the woods, with a remarkably high wall and higher monument. The family returned to Europe. He could not have imagined how dead he would be in a few years, and all the more dead and forgotten for being buried under such a mass of gloomy stone, where not even memory could get at him without a crowbar. Ah! poor man, with that last end of his! However, he may have been the worthiest of mortals for aught that I know. From the mountain-top we got a view of the whole city; the flat, fertile, extensive island; the noble sea of the St. Lawrence swelling into lakes; the mountains about St. Hyacinth, and in Vermont and New York; and the mouth of the Ottawa in the west, overlooking that St. Ann's where the voyageur sings his "part-ing hymn," and bids adieu to civilization—a name, thanks to Moore's verses, the most suggestive of poetic associations of any in Canada. We, too, climbed the hill which Cartier, first of white men, ascended, and named Montreal (the 3d of October, O. S., 1535), and, like him, "we saw the said river as far as we could see, *grand, large, et spacieux,* going to the southwest," toward that land whither Donnacona had told the discoverer that he had been a month's journey from Canada, where there grew "*force Canelle et Girofle,*" much cinnamon and cloves, and where also, as the natives told him, were three great lakes and afterward *une mer douce*—a sweet sea—*de laquelle n'est mention avoir vu le bout,* of which there is no mention to have seen the end. But instead of an Indian town far in the interior of a new world, with guides to show us where the river came from, we found a splendid and bustling stone-built city of white men, and only a few squalid Indians offered to sell us baskets at the Lachine Railroad Depot, and Hochelaga is, perchance, but the fancy name of an engine company or an eating-house.

We left Montreal Wednesday, the 2d of October, late in the afternoon. In the La Prairie cars the Yankees made themselves merry, imitating the cries of the charette-drivers to perfection, greatly to the amusement of some French-Canadian travellers, and they kept it up all the way to Boston. I saw one person on board the boat at St. John's, and one or two more elsewhere in Canada, wearing homespun gray greatcoats, or capotes, with conical and comical hoods, which fell back between their shoulders like small bags, ready to be turned up over the head when occasion required, though a hat usurped that place now. They looked as if they would be convenient and proper enough as long as the coats were new and tidy, but would soon come to have a beggarly and unsightly look, akin to rags and dust-holes. We reached Burlington early in the morning, where the Yankees tried to pass off their Canada coppers, but the news-boys knew better. Returning through the Green Mountains, I was reminded that I had not seen in Canada such brilliant autumnal tints as I had previously seen in Vermont. Perhaps there was not yet so great and sudden a contrast with the summer heats in the former country as in these mountain valleys. As we were passing through Ashburnham, by a new white house which stood at some distance in a field, one passenger exclaimed, so that all in the car could hear him, "There, there's not so good a house as that in all Canada!" I did not much wonder at his remark, for there is a neatness, as well as evident prosperity, a certain elastic easiness of circumstances, so to speak, when not rich, about a New England house, as if the proprietor could at least afford to make repairs in the spring, which the Canadian houses do not suggest. Though of stone, they are no better constructed than a stone barn would be with us; the only building, except the chateau, on which money and taste are expended, being the church. In Canada an ordinary New England house would be mistaken for the chateau, and while every village here contains at least several gentlemen or "squires," *there* there is but one to a seigniory.

I got home this Thursday evening, having spent just one week in Canada and travelled eleven hundred miles. The whole expense of this journey, including two guide-books and a map, which cost one dollar twelve and a half cents, was twelve dollars seventy-five cents. I do not suppose that I have seen all British America; that could not be done by a cheap excursion, unless it were a cheap excursion to the Icy Sea, as seen by Hearne or McKenzie, and then, no doubt, some interesting features would be omitted. I wished to go a little way behind that word *Canadense,* of which naturalists make such frequent use; and I should like still right well to make a longer excursion on foot through the wilder parts of Canada, which perhaps might be called *Iter Canadense.*

THE LITERARY NATURALIST SERIES celebrates some of America's noted naturalists—those writers who saw the natural world as the settings for some of their most inspired life experiences. Literary naturalists transcend political boundaries, social concerns, and historical milieus; they speak for what Henry Beston called the "other nations" of the planet. Today, the results of these writers acquire an urgency and increasing importance as wild places become fewer, farther between and increasingly scarce, and perhaps even sacred. This collection of books and writers celebrates both a precious body of work, and a fundamental truth: that nature counts as a model, a guide to how we can live in our quickly changing world.

OTHER TITLES IN THE SERIES

Alaska Days with John Muir
The Cruise of the Corwin
The Maine Woods